Using the Overhead Projector

J R H JONES

Heinemann Educational Books
London

Heinemann Educational Books Ltd
22 Bedford Square, London WC1B 3HH

LONDON EDINBURGH MELBOURNE AUCKLAND
HONG KONG SINGAPORE KUALA LUMPUR
NEW DELHI IBADAN NAIROBI
JOHANNESBURG EXETER (NH) KINGSTON
PORT OF SPAIN

First published 1982

British Library Cataloguing in Publication Data

Jones, J.R.H.
Using the overhead projector. – (Practical language teaching; 8)
1. English language – Study and teaching – Foreign students 2. English language – Study and teaching – Audio-visual aids 3. Overhead projection
I. Title II. Series
428.2'4'078 PE1128.A2

ISBN 0-435-28972-1

Illustrated by The Parkway Group from the author's own drawings and visual aids.
Set in 10 on 12 point Times by The Yale Press Limited, London SE25
Printed and bound in Great Britain by Biddles Ltd, Guildford, Surrey

Contents

Preface

The overhead projector has been defined as 'a well-lit horizontal surface where mugs of coffee may conveniently be placed' (*EFL Gazette,* 1980). This book is for any language teacher who has ever wondered what other purposes it might serve.

The examples throughout the book are designed for the teaching of English as a foreign language at every level, from beginners and children to advanced students and adults. The topics cover general courses and English for Special Purposes (ESP). But the methods involved, and in particular the weight given to the visual element in modern language teaching, should be of interest to a much wider audience.

The materials are also intended to be *cost-effective.* In other words, they are easy and cheap to make, and they perform a real pedagogical function. Anything else has been excluded. The materials are also thoroughly good fun to make and use, as I hope you will find.

JRHJ Oslo.

Acknowledgements

The authors and publishers wish to thank the following for permission to reproduce their material and for providing illustrations and photographs:
Fig. 5 Elite Optics Ltd, Cardiff; Fig. 6 and Fig. 79 Leybold-Heraeus GMBH, West Germany; Fig. 7 by kind permission of 3M (UK) Ltd; Fig. 12 from *Politics in Britain* by Peter Bromhead (published by Evans, 1979); Fig. 13 from *Streamline English: Departures* by Bernard Hartley and Peter Viney (published by Oxford University Press) (c) OUP 1978; Fig. 17 by kind permission of Transart Ltd. East Chadley Lane. Godmanchester, Huntingdon, Cambridgeshire PE18 8AU; Fig. 23 from *Success with English Coursebook 2* (Penguin Education 1968) reproduction by permission of Penguin Books Ltd, copyright (c) Geoffrey Broughton; Fig. 24 from *Britain Today* by R. Musman (published by Longman 1977); Figs. 25, 34, 78 from *Selections from Modern English Teacher* edited by H. Moorwood (published by Longman 1978); Fig. 57 reproduced by kind permission of Kawasaki and Honda Ltd; Fig. 66 from *First Things First* by L. G. Alexander (published by Longman 1967); Fig. 72 from *Under Milk Wood* by Dylan Thomas (published by J. M. Dent Ltd); Fig. 76 from *Modern Language Classroom Techniques* by E. D. Allen and R. M. Valette (published by Harcourt Brace Jovanovich, Inc 1972); Fig. 80 by kind permission of ESA Creative Learning Ltd; Fig. 81 and Fig. 83 from *The Overhead Projector* by Judith Wilkinson (published by The British Council, 1979); Fig. 82 by kind permission of Technical Animations Ltd, 3 Osiers Road, Wandsworh, London SW19 1NL.

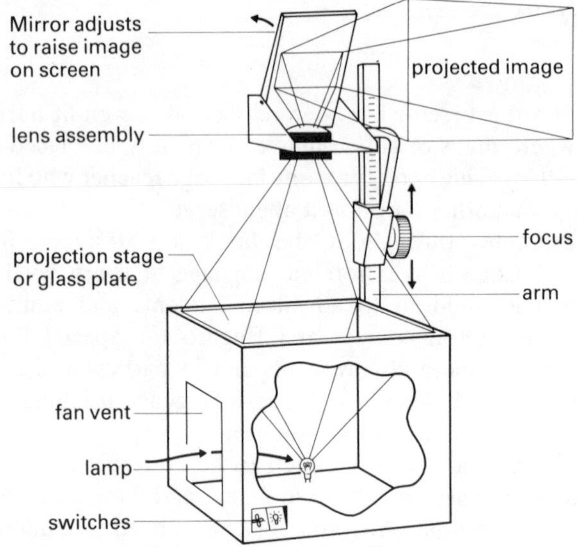

Figure 1 Fan-cooled overhead projector

Figure 2 Operator faces audience

Machine and Materials

1 *What Can an Overhead Projector Do?*

An overhead projector simply shines a light through a transparency the size of a sheet of notepaper, projecting it on to an ordinary film screen (see Figure 1). The operator has the transparency right way up, and horizontal, in front of him (see Figure 2). It can be moved, altered or written on while he faces his audience. The audience see the image enlarged on the screen behind the operator. The picture on the screen is sufficiently clear in ordinary daylight. Blackout is unnecessary and even ordinary curtains are only needed in bright direct sunlight or with a darkish transparency.

Most overhead projectors are quite heavy and it takes both hands to carry one. If there was an overhead projector screwed down tight in every classroom – as blackboards are – more people would use them. But what justification is there for carrying this fairly bulky piece of equipment to the classroom if it is to be used for perhaps five minutes of a lesson? Frankly, if you are just going to write on it during the course of the lesson – none at all. The blackboard is more convenient for that, unless you want to avoid turning your back on your audience. But the projector wins in the following cases:

(a) Preparation of more ambitious writing and pictures can be done *beforehand* on transparencies and shown in class ready-made, which saves class time.
(b) This also gives you a chance, if you need it, to prepare your pictures in privacy. The class only see the finished work.
(c) Transparencies can be *reused* and maps, diagrams and substitution tables filed for next year's class.

(d) It is easier to *conceal* something on the projector. You can reveal the transcript of a dictation passage when it is needed, and not before.

The overhead projector is particularly good with *pictures*. It has the following advantages over 'pictureboards' such as the magnetboard, flannelboard, or pictures stuck on to the chalkboard:

(a) The working surface is *horizontal*. Things are less likely to fall off. They do not have to be magnetized or made sticky in any way.
(b) As images are *magnified* on the screen, they can be drawn conveniently small, and still be clearly seen.
(c) As images on transparencies are generally translucent, they can be *combined* by superimposition, as in Figure 3. In particular, colour and line can be combined, as in Figure 4.
(d) Objects can conveniently be *silhouetted* on the overhead projector. This gives a further range of dramatic possibilities. See Chapter 9.

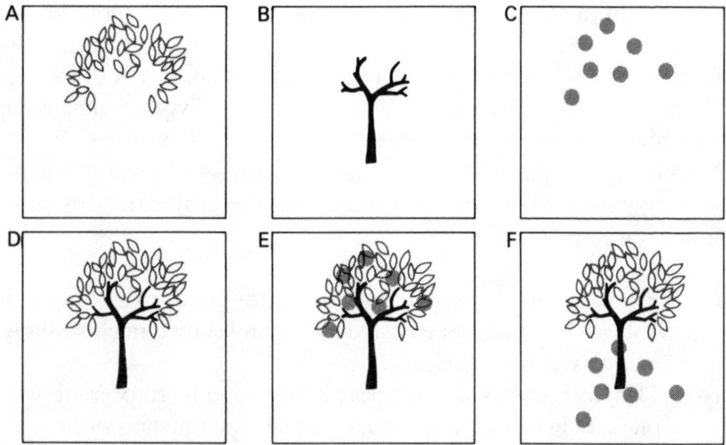

Figure 3 Superimposition
Trace elements of (E) on to three separate transparencies (A, B, C). Different combinations give (D) and (F). Useful for illustrating seasons and tenses: It's autumn. The leaves have just fallen.

Figure 4 Colour and line combined
Indian can be drawn on separate transparency and moved across the coloured background.

Like the various pictureboards, and unlike static wallcharts, the overhead projector gives you the option of building up a picture *gradually*, element by element. This means that the class can be more closely involved in the development of a picture than if you served it up to them complete. They can *guess* what will happen next. You may even involve them further by asking them to *decide* what will happen next.

On the other hand, the overhead projector is not strong on realism. It is possible to *photocopy* realistic material on to transparencies (see the section on 'Copiers' in Chapter 3), but it is cartoons and diagrams which are the overhead projector's strong point.

It is possible to show *movement,* through articulated models, polarized light, and the other amazing equipment outlined in Chapter 13. Or one can simply and usefully move about the elements of a picture and create movement that way. One can cause the leaves to fall from the tree in Figure 3, for instance. The great appeal to the teacher is that one can make one's *own* visuals with very simple material. They will be flexible, effective, attractive, and quick to make.

At this point, if you have never laid hands on an overhead projector, perhaps you should now find out what keys, janitors, official forms or secret passwords are required to get one out of a cupboard and into the classroom. The hardest task will then be over, and you will be able to use and enjoy the ideas in the rest of this book.

2 *Choosing and Maintaining an Overhead Projector*

This chapter is in two parts. The first deals with the points a language teacher needs to look for if he is buying an overhead projector. The second part tells you how to look after an overhead projector once you have got one.

2.1 CHOOSING AN OVERHEAD PROJECTOR

The following points are based on the standards set out in User Specification 3 (USPEC 3), used by the Experimental Development Unit of the National Council for Educational Technology in Britain. Their reports on individual machines are available from the National Audio-Visual Aids Centre (NAVAC), at Paxton Place, Gipsy Road, London SE27 9SR. The reports also take into account general safety requirements, which are not considered here.

2.1.1. FAN-COOLED PROJECTORS

Most overhead projectors have a fan-cooled lamp in a 'biscuit tin' at the bottom. This is the kind of projector which is illustrated in Figure 5. The 'biscuit tin' makes the projector a bulky piece of equipment, often nine or ten kilos, which is a reasonable two-handed load. Having to move an overhead projector is undesirable, for this and other reasons.

(a) Teachers are discouraged from using the machine: they often have their hands full on the way to a lesson already.

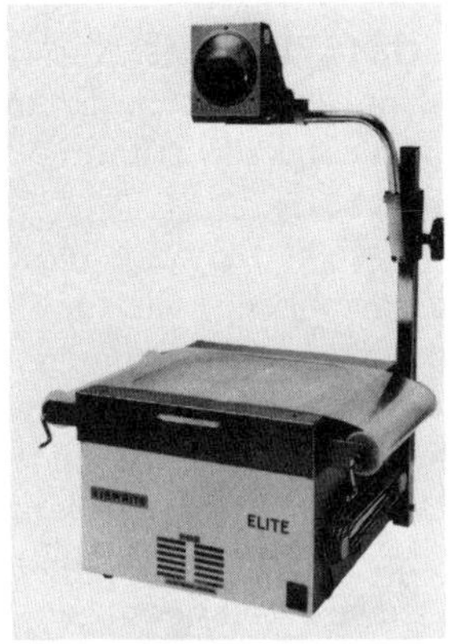

Figure 5 Fan-cooled projector with acetate roll

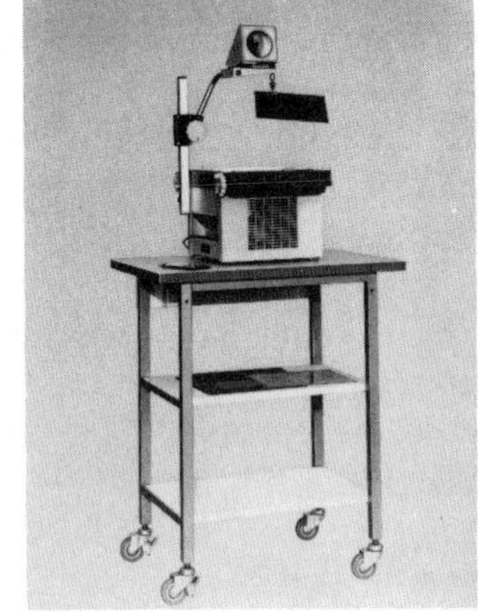

Figure 6 Projector trolley

(b) It is much more convenient if both the projector and its screen have permanent places in the classroom so that the machine can just be switched on instead of requiring setting up and adjusting.

(c) If the projector is moved while the lamp is hot, the filament will suffer.

Ideally, therefore, a projector would be set in a built-in teacher's desk in the room where it was to be used. There would be a permanent screen, and a concealed cable to the machine, which no one could trip over. Failing this, the projector could be locked in a cupboard in the same room. Failing this, a number of rooms on the same floor could share a projector, wheeled around on a suitable trolley, such as the model in Figure 6. The last resort is to have teachers manhandling the machines up and down stairs between staffroom and classroom.

The clearest picture, and the longest lamp life, are produced by lamps running off *low voltages* of twelve or twenty-four volts. However, the necessary transformer adds greatly to the cost and weight of the machine. If the projector has to be carried, a lighter model might be preferable.

Noise can be a problem with fan-cooled projectors. A decibel level of fifty dBA might be acceptable for many purposes, but the language classroom demands a quiet machine. There are various models which produce forty-five dBA or less. Listen to the machine for yourself if you can: pitch can be as irritating as volume.

Scatter papers around the machine to see if they are blown about by the *draught* from the fan: there have been models in the past whose vents have required remodelling after complaints about this.

The *cooler* the machine, the better. The temperature rise on the glass plate (the 'projection stage') when the machine is in use should not be more than 50°C and many projectors are available with rises in the 30–40°C range, which makes it easier to write during projection without the ink drying up and disappearing.

Lamp life is extended if a *thermal switch* is incorporated. This keeps the cooling fan running until the lamp is properly cooled.

2.1.2 REFLECTOR PROJECTORS

The other type of projector is shown in Figure 7. Its lamp is in the assembly above the glass plate. Light passes down through the transparency and is then reflected back up to the lenses by a mirror in the base. One has to be particularly careful not to scratch this mirror.

Figure 7 Reflector projector

The absence of a fan makes these projectors smaller and lighter. They are usually supplied with a convenient carrying case, comparable in size and weight with an electric typewriter of the more portable sort. They are also completely silent. The only drawback is that because the light has to pass through the transparency twice, the image tends to be less bright.

2.1.3 THE IMAGE ON THE SCREEN

The standard overhead projector has a 25 × 25 cm glass plate. There are also larger 'A4' or 30 × 30 cm models, but they tend to be heavier and project an image which is less bright.

A 25 × 25 cm projector normally stands about 2.4 m from its screen. At this distance the projected image is about 1.5 m square. Some models are designed to project an image of this size from a shorter distance: this can be an advantage in cramped circumstances.

The image should be bright enough for use in normal daylight. An output of 1400 lumens is supposed to provide sufficient brightness at the centre of the screen (1800 lumens is rather more usual; 2000 lumens gives a very bright picture). Brightness is bound to fall off towards the edges, and edge-to-edge brightness is not critical in the applications described in this book.

Many machines provide two levels of brightness. The principle is the same as for many slide projectors. The less bright level is for normal use and maximizes bulb life; the brighter level is for difficult lighting conditions or poor transparencies.

The NAVAC reports also take into account the resolution and contrast of the picture, requiring that the former be eight lines per millimetre at the centre of the picture. Brightness and clarity are best judged informally by putting a poor transparency on the projector. To take an extreme case, if a darkish photocopy of newsprint is readable ten metres away from the screen, nothing more is going to be asked of the machine than that.

The glass plate obviously needs to be kept clean if the picture is to stay bright. It is a good idea to keep the glass covered when not in use: this prevents chalk dusk from settling on it. It helps if there is access between the underside of the glass plate on a fan-cooled projector, and the fresnel lens beneath (which directs light into the lens assembly). This allows one to spring-clean from time to time.

2.2. CLASSROOM MANAGEMENT

Figure 8 shows an ideal arrangement for an overhead projector in a classroom. The screen is visible throughout the room, allowing various seating arrangements. If the class were working in groups, for instance, and one group were using the overhead projector, they could be out of everyone else's way in the corner of the room.

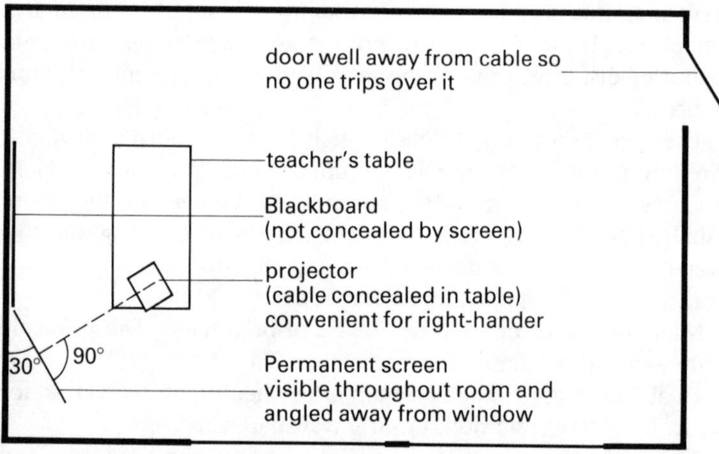

Figure 8 Ideal arrangement for projector and screen

At the same time, the projector is within easy reach of the teacher's usual position, yet sitting or standing at it, he would not obscure the screen.

The screen is angled away from light from the windows. It can be used in conjunction with the blackboard.

The screen is also hooked back at the bottom (see Figure 9) so that the projected image is absolutely square.

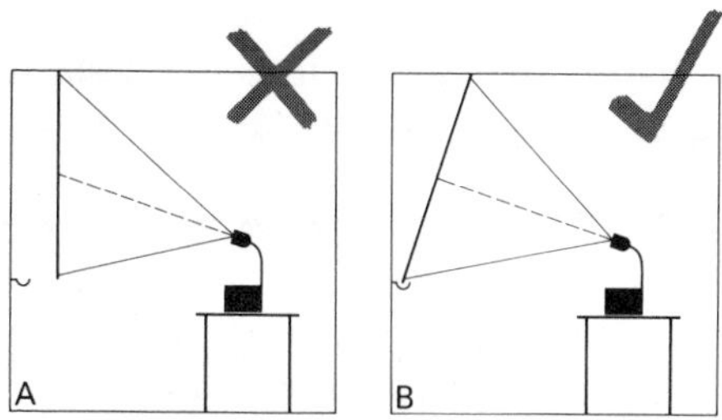

Figure 9 Getting a square image
Ideally, the screen should tilt back as in B, so that the screen is square to the projector. In A, there will be 'keystoning': the bottom of the projected image will be narrower than the top.

Most classrooms are not like this, however. The screen (or the back of a roller map used as a substitute) hangs directly over the blackboard. This does not matter unless you want to use them simultaneously (see Chapter 12 for ideas on using the overhead projector in combination with other aids). If you do, perhaps there is a convenient patch of pale wall beside the blackboard: this will do perfectly well as a temporary screen. If you have a *whiteboard*, you can of course project directly on to that, as long as it is clean.

Nor does it matter if the screen is directly behind the projector, as long as you project fairly high (by tilting the lens assembly shown in Figure 1). You may have to crouch a bit, or even sit down. (This is what many handbooks advise, but many people find that sitting down cramps their teaching style.) If you are still casting an annoying shadow (Figure 10), it may be necessary to sacrifice part of the illuminated area by blocking off the light with a mask on the glass screen of the projector, as in Figure 11.

Figure 10 If you cast a shadow . . .

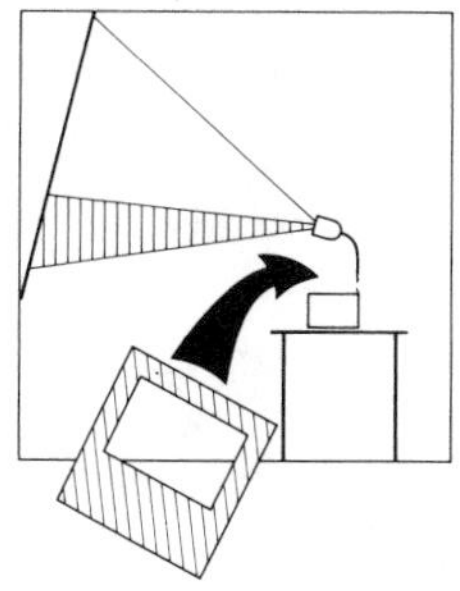

Figure 11 . . . Make a permanent mask

Nor does it matter if there is no teacher's desk. Any flat desk or table will do, as long as you can reach it to operate it while teaching.

Nothing really matters at all, unless the projector cable has to pass across the doorway to reach the socket. In this case, for safety's sake, do not plug in until everyone is seated, and try and remember to unplug the projector before people leave their seats. Make sure there is plenty of cable, using an extension cord if necessary, so that if anyone trips over it, they will not pull the machine off its table.

2.3 OPERATION

Find the on/off switch (usually marked, but sometimes a plain touch-bar along the operator's side of the machine). Project a transparency to check that the machine is focused on the screen: if not, focus by winding the lens assembly up or down its arm (see Figure 1).

You will probably find it most effective to use the machine in short bursts to present simple graphic ideas. Leaving the projector on for long periods dissipates the dramatic effect.

A good habit to get into is to position a transparency before switching on, and not to meddle with it thereafter. Images which shuffle about to no apparent purpose are very wearisome and distracting for the audience.

If the projector has to be moved at the end of a lesson, give it time to cool down first. This process is speeded up if you can leave the fan on with the lamp switched off. On machines with thermal switches, the fan runs automatically until the lamp is cool.

2.4 MAINTENANCE

There are two aspects of maintenance which it is wise to know something about: cleaning the glass plate and changing the bulb.

If there is chalk dust on the glass plate, wipe it off with a clean, dry cloth, *not* the blackboard eraser. (It happens, believe me!) If the glass plate needs more thorough cleaning from time to time, do this while the machine is unplugged and cool.

Keep the projector covered – even a piece of paper over the glass plate will help – and away from chalk dust when not in use, if this is possible.

Spare projection bulbs come in little holders to help you to change them without touching them. (The quartz in the glass of the lamp is apparently affected by acid in the skin pores: the quartz turns milky and eventually bursts.) If you do get your fingerprints on a bulb, you can wipe them off with methylated spirits before anyone sees them.

Bulbs go very rarely, if properly treated, but they go at the worst times. Therefore find out now, and not in the heat of battle, who you get a spare one from. And find out who (probably someone quite different!) can show you how to change it. It is one of those jobs which seems very difficult unless you have actually done it once. Then it seems easy.

3 *What Materials Do You Need?*

There are many materials on the market which are specifically designed for use on overhead projector transparencies. Some are essential, and others are useful only if you have the time and inclination to prettify. In this chapter the main types of material, including transparencies made on copiers, are described and assessed. There is a list of suppliers on pages 89-92.

3.1 PAPERS AND PENS

3.1.1 TRANSPARENT SHEETS

The usual commercially available sheets are cellofilm and acetate, but a cheap alternative is cleared X-ray film, which is thick, bluish, and available from some hospitals (see Best, 1968).

Cellofilm is as cheap as paper and can be written on with all kinds of pens. It is ideal for trying out new ideas, or for use by the whole class. It is also flimsy, liable to curl on the projector, of variable optical quality and cannot be satisfactorily cleaned. It is most useful to think of it as disposable.

Acetate is more expensive (from 5p upwards for a single A4 sheet at the time of writing). It is stronger than cellofilm, clearer, cleanable and does not curl, even if cut into smaller pieces. However, only certain pens will write satisfactorily on acetate (see following section).

3.1.2 PENS

Water- and spirit-based pens for the overhead projector produce a translucent line (i.e. you can see the colour when it is projected).

'Medium thickness' pens are fine enough for the purposes in this book. If you also limit your colour range to a palette of black, blue, red and green, this will keep your line work bold and clear. But this is a matter of taste and style.

Water-based ('soluble' or 'T-type') pens are erasable from acetate with a damp cloth, but cellofilm wrinkles when dampened. Water-based pens are useful for less permanent work.

Spirit-based ('K-type') pens are for permanent work: they are erasable from acetate only with a solvent such as white spirit. The pen manufacturers produce various proprietary solvents, impregnated tissues, erasers and correction pens.

Lines can also be drawn on acetate with a draughtsman's pen and Indian ink, if this is needed for maps and other fine, detailed work.

A wax pencil, erasable with a dry cloth, is useful for impermanent additions. (See Satchwell, 1972 or McRae, 1975, for details.)

3.1.3 COLOUR SHEETS

Areas of colour can be added to line drawings with water- or spirit-based 'magic markers', or thick felt pens, but these project rather blotchily.

Self-adhesive colour film can give a professional and attractive finish. Choose lighter colours, so that lines and writing will project clearly *through* areas of colour. Colour film is expensive and takes time to apply properly. Add it to line drawings only if there is some pedagogical point, as in Figure 12 and Figure 13.

In Figure 12, the coloured shapes are easy to measure up and cut out of the colour sheet. The alternative is to place the line drawing over the colour sheet and firmly draw the outline of the area to be coloured, using a pencil. This will leave an impression on the colour sheet, which you can cut round with scissors.

For more complex shapes, as in Figure 13, cut out a slightly larger area of colour than needed, peel off the backing paper, and attach the colour to the transparency as in Figure 14 (A). Then cut it to the exact dimensions with a craft knife, scoring the colour sheet lightly so that the acetate beneath is not cut through. Lift off the excess colour with the side of the knife blade. This results in a very satisfactory job, but takes time. Acceptable simplified substitutes are shown in Figure 15.

How the British electoral system works. General Election Results 1945–74

	Conservative		Labour		Liberal	
	Votes %	Seats	Votes %	Seats	Votes %	Seats
July 1945	39.8	213	47.8 *	393	9	12
Feb. 1950	43.5	298	46.1 *	315	9	9
Oct. 1951	48.0 *	321	48.8	295	2·5	8
May 1955	49.7 *	344	46.4	277	2·7	6
Oct. 1959	49.4 *	365	43.8	258	5·9	6
Oct. 1964	43.4	304	44.1 *	317	11·2	9
March 1966	41.9	253	49.9 *	363	8·5	12
Oct. 1970	46.1 *	330	43.0	287	7·7	6
Feb. 1974	37.8	297	37.1 *	301	19·3	14
Oct. 1974	35.8	277	39.2 *	319	18·3	13

Figure 12 Colour for contrast and cohesion
Translucent colour patches are added to a textbook diagram (Peter Bromhead, Politics in Britain, *(Evans, 1979), p. 7,) to identify and contrast the three political parties. Stars have also been added to show the winner of each election.*

Figure 13 Colour added to textbook figures to help identification (*Pictures simplified from B. Hartley and P. Viney,* Streamline English Departures (*OUP, 1978*), *Lesson 4.*)

Figure 14 Applying self-adhesive colour
(A) *Colour sheet, cut larger than needed, is applied to transparency.*
(B) *Colour sheet is cut to exact size with craft knife.*

Figure 15 Colour shapes in your own pictures
(A) *Commercially produced colour shapes, (circles) and . . .*
(B) *Simple cut-out colour shapes. Both to present comparative forms of adjectives.*
(C) *Some simple shapes are recognizable without line additions.*
(D) *After drawing a picture, stick on a quite arbitrary colour shape for emphasis, contrast with other figures, or just decoration.*

Non-adhesive colour sheets are also available: theatre gels for stage lighting are a relatively inexpensive source of these. Whole sheets can be used to give an overall background of one colour, but use light colours, so that line drawings and writing show through.

Another use of non-adhesive colour is to cut out a number of simple shapes, such as squares and circles, which can be moved about on the surface of a transparency. These either draw attention to certain areas of the transparency, or provide colour options (e.g. to practise *The cup was blue*, or *Now it's yellow*, with beginner's classes).

Adhesive patterned sheets can be found, printed with stripes, dots, log-paper grids, musical staffs, pie charts and so forth. It is economical to reuse these rather expensive materials. One way is to make any additions in water-based inks so that they can be erased later. Another is to tape the adhesive sheet to the underside of another transparency. The additions can then be made to the top sheet. The two sheets can be stored separately, but reused together at a later date.

3.1.4 STORAGE

Acetate sheets in standard sizes can simply be punched and filed. *Interleaves* of *ordinary paper* will:

(a) help to protect the acetates,
(b) make it easier to see the individual transparency while flicking through the file,
(c) teaching notes can be written on them.

If the interleaf is a *photocopy* of the transparency, it makes it easier to put the transparency back in the right place after use.

Acetate sheets can also be *mounted*. A standard card mount is shown in Figure 16. There are files big enough to take forty of these mounts, which are 31.5 × 31.5 cm, but I store them on open shelves. See Wilkinson (1979:62) for files.

There are *glassine envelopes*, which just take a standard sheet, plus a margin for file holes. The transparency can be projected in its envelope.

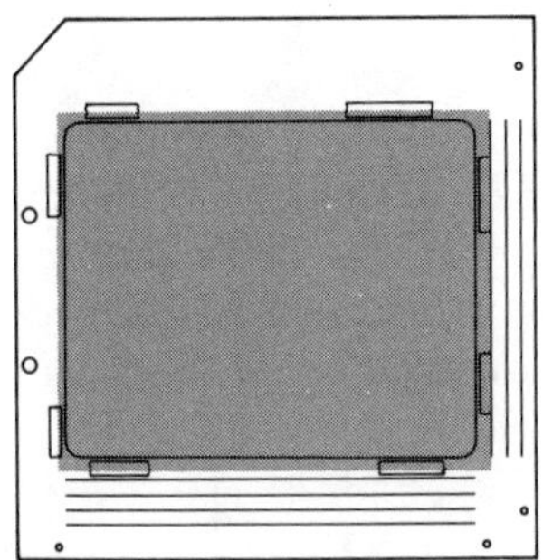

Figure 16 Commercial mount (20 × 25 cm aperture)
Acetate (shaded here) is taped to upper *side of mount to give smooth working surface. Commercial mounts have file and registration holes and room for notes.*

Cellofilm transparencies must be protected and stiffened in one of the above ways if they are to be preserved. Some schools, notably East Sheen Primary School in London, have built up useful and very attractive *libraries* of the best pictures which their pupils have drawn on to cellofilm.

If you have a set of transparencies which you wish to keep and show in a given order, the *Flipatran* system (Figure 17) provides compact and convenient storage. The *Cellobinder* is a similar system.

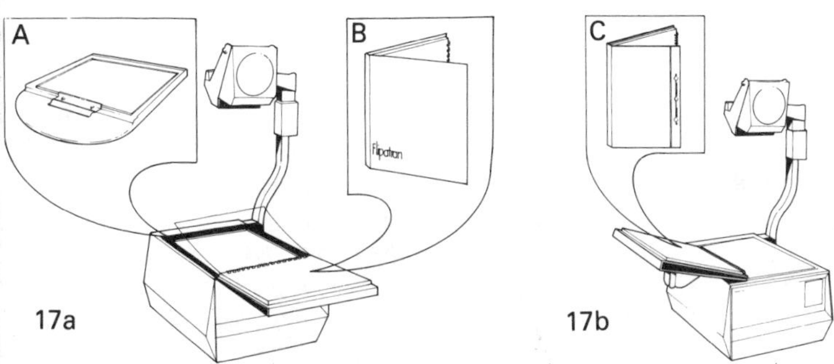

Figure 17 Flipatran storage system
17a Flipatran
Frame (A) supports filed transparencies (B). Not suitable for use on reflector projectors.
17b Flipatran 3
Recommended by the makers for use with any overhead projector.

3.2 THE ACETATE ROLL

Most fan-cooled projectors are supplied with a roll of acetate attached, as in Figure 5. This can be left in place while sheet transparencies are projected. If the transparencies are tucked under the roll (Figure 18), the roll can be used for additions *during* the lesson, without dirtying the sheet transparency.

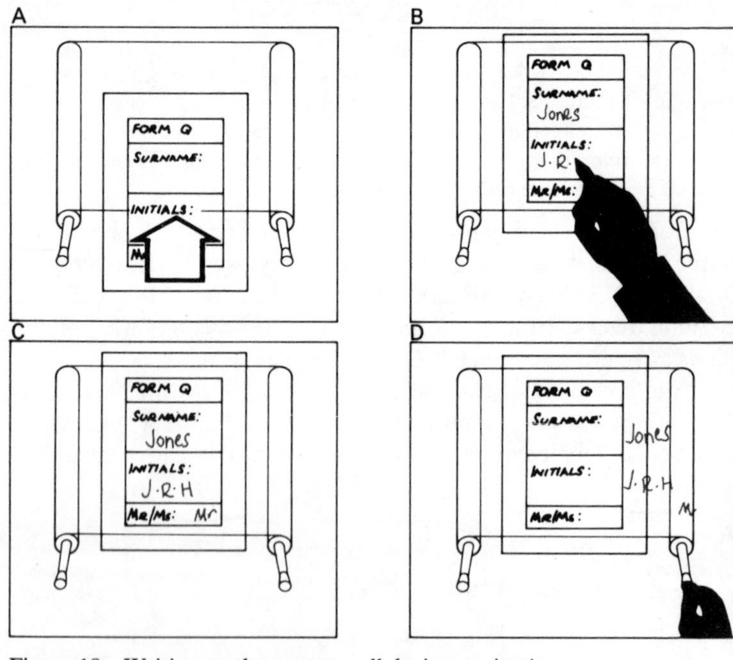

Figure 18 Writing on the acetate roll during projection
(A) *Slide a transparency* under *the roll.*
(B) *Make any additions on the acetate roll.*
(C) *They will appear to be on the transparency itself.*
(D) *They can be removed by winding the roll, leaving the transparency clear for reuse.*

It is, of course, also possible to use the roll for preparing material *before* the lesson. The relative advantages of roll and sheet transparencies are akin to the relative advantages of film-strips and slides: with the acetate roll, as with a filmstrip, you can be sure that your notes and pictures will appear in the right order.

This may be important in a lecture, for instance. But for flexibility and, above all, for permitting the reuse of the individual pictures in other combinations in other lessons, it is more convenient to draw and store material on individual transparencies. If the ordering of these transparencies is critical, put a sticky label on each one and number them clearly.

3.3 LETTERING

Make an underlay as a guide to your own lettering, like the one in Figure 19. It does not take long to make, and it will show you:

(a) how big your projection area is,
(b) how to keep your lettering straight and even,
(c) how to make sure that your lettering is always big enough for everyone to read.

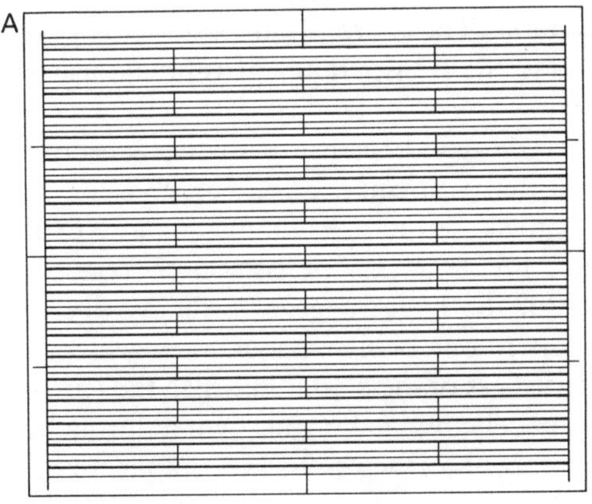

Figure 19 Guidesheet for lettering
(A) *Guidesheet, showing limits of standard 20 × 25cm aperture, is taped to underside of design.*
(B) *Lettering for medium thickness projector pen: guidelines enlarged from (A).*

If there are any problems of layout, put a sheet of ordinary paper over the underlay (which should be in black ink on white paper so that you can see it through another sheet of paper). Rough out your lettering in thick pencil. After adjustments, write out the finished transparency with a medium-thick pen, using the rough draft and underlay as a guide.

There are also various ways of projecting *typescript* (see Waller, 1978) if you want things to look extra professional.

Typing directly on to acetate with a special carbon paper or ribbon (see Best, 1968) is a quick way of copying out a lengthy piece of writing such as a dictation passage. However, only the 'jumbo' type sizes available on some 'golf ball' typewriters are big enough to project clearly. With normal type sizes, even the capital letters are a bit small for completely clear projection. And in any case, it seems a pity to type in uniform black when you can write your own lettering in colour.

Stencilling is neat and quick if you are used to it.

Dry transfer projection lettering is available in a limited range of styles and colours. (These are plastic letters, like Letraset, which are transferred to the transparency by rubbing: use an underlay to guide you.)

The lettering designed for use with the overhead projector is translucent, so that you can see the colour when it is projected. However, if you wanted to use one of the more exotic type styles (fancy Gothic, for example, or computer-style typefaces), you could use one of the huge range of ordinary dry transfer styles. They are cheaper, but being opaque they will project in black silhouette, regardless of the colour in which they are printed.

You could conceivably make your own lettering by cutting each individual letter out of self-adhesive colour film, if the spirit moved you.

Lettering is all great fun, but hand lettering, kept straight and even by an underlay, is fine for most purposes. One is *teaching*, after all, not competing with the advertising industry, and hand lettering is all that most of us have time for.

3.4 COPIERS

There are various ways of making transparent photocopies. So various, in fact, that I will simply say that if you have a copier of any kind, even a spirit duplicator, it is worth reading the instruction manual, or getting in touch with the manufacturers, to see if advice or materials for making transparencies are available.

There are guides by Powell (1964) and Satchwell (1972) which give a lot of useful advice on copying for the overhead projector. There are also various manufacturers' guides on individual processes. Tecnifax's *Diazochrome Projectuals for Visual Communication* (1963) is good and clear on dyeline machines, for instance. 3M's *Op Art* (1965) describes heat copiers, among other things. Kodak's *Preparing Transparencies* deals with copying through photographic techniques.

Only photography produces half-tone: transparencies produced by other methods do not give intermediate degrees of shading.

Colour is possible with all the three methods mentioned above. There are special papers for heat copiers which will give a coloured line on a clear background, or a black or transparent line on a coloured background, all from the same black-on-white original.

If you make a photocopied transparency of a textbook page, or a handout, you can direct attention easily. Instead of laboriously explaining the page and line number to a class, you can simply point. Even if the print is too small to read in projection, this helps the class to find their place.

You can conceal parts of the text, to draw attention to the rest, where the answer to your comprehension question may be lurking, for instance. You can project a readable text for a limited time, to control reading speed. See Brims (1978) for some useful suggestions.

In addition, photocopied transparencies are valuable wherever *realism* is required. It has already been said that realism is not the overhead projector's strong point, but newspaper styles, for instance, can be analysed with the help of transparencies of cuttings. Many technical drawings can be photocopied directly: the projected image will be big enough for everyone to see the details. Transparencies can be made of people or places which you want to be identified, and which you do not think you could draw. These realistic images can, as we shall see, be combined with your own pictures, colour and lettering.

Finally, a pupil's work can be copied on to a transparency to exemplify points about layout, common errors, marking, good work and so on, as in Figure 20.

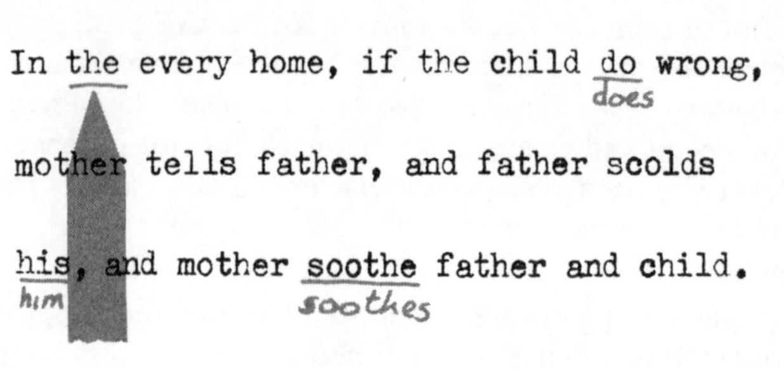

Figure 20 Correcting homework on a transparency

In classes with a medical content, an ordinary radiograph, if not too dark, can be projected on the overhead projector, but you will probably need to draw the curtains (McRae, 1975). Radiographs for the overhead projector are available, but they are very expensive.

3.5 SUMMARY

For the ideas in this book, all you really *need* are acetate sheets and medium thickness water-based pens. Cellofilm, spirit-based pens, and self-adhesive colour sheets in light green, light red, and light blue would be very useful extras. If you have a copier, find out how it does transparencies.

The other materials described above are fun if you have the time, money and inclination. I am not sure whether their use greatly enhances the *teaching* value of one's transparencies.

4 *But I Can't Draw!*

You can't draw. Good: this is the aid for you. As all the materials are transparent, you can borrow material from anywhere, within the bounds of the copyright laws, by *tracing* it.

4.1 TRACING FOR PROJECTION

Remember that you are copying from books and papers designed to be read in the hand, and these images will project to poster size at the end of a room. The transparency therefore needs to be bolder and simpler than the book image.

Maps are a good example. In Figure 21, Copy A would project as weak and hesitant: the fine, conscientious line would appear uncertain and inaccurate. Copy B is in a thicker pen and the artist has simplified the outline and straightened each section of the line.

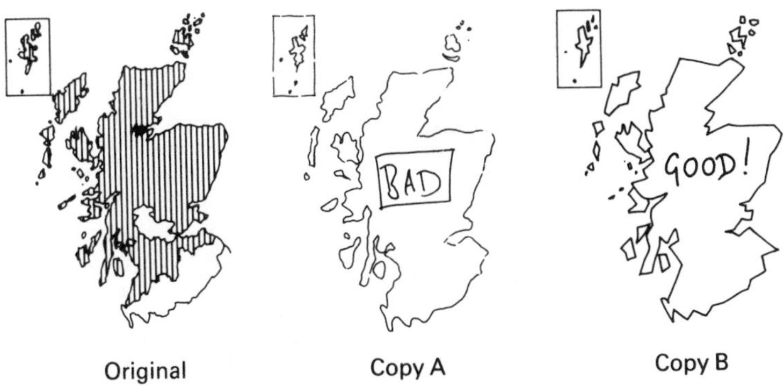

Figure 21 Tracing boldly

The technique is like 'joining the dots': you imagine numbered dots at salient points along the coast, and then join them up with firm, straight lines. The second map will look clear and confident in projection, and if some accuracy has been sacrificed, well, no one is going to use an overhead projector transparency to find his way round Scotland!

The same goes for pictures, especially if the original has a delicate, amusing line like Quentin Blake's illustration in Figure 22. If you try and reproduce this on the projector, it will look wiggly and uncertain. The safest thing to do is to simplify by cutting out details which are not relevant to the teaching point (prepositions of place, etc., see Broughton, 1969:96). Straighten and join up the important lines. In other words, let the transparency *state* the shapes which the delicate original *hints* at.

Figure 22 Make pictures simple and bold for projection
(Original from G. Broughton, Success with English. *Coursebook 2 (Penguin, 1969), p.96. Drawn by Quentin Blake.)*

4.2 TRACING FOR REPEATED USE

Once you have made a transparency, you can reuse it as often as you wish. Try, therefore, to make the transparency as *generally useful as possible*. Remove any details which would prevent the image from being used in other situations, or in combination with other elements.

For example, suppose you want a picture of a character in the textbook you are using. You want that character to be recognizable, but you also want to make a single drawing which can be used in combination with other elements to illustrate any situation in the course. Simplify him as in Figure 23, and the figure will last you the whole book through, and then live on to be used in quite different lessons in the future.

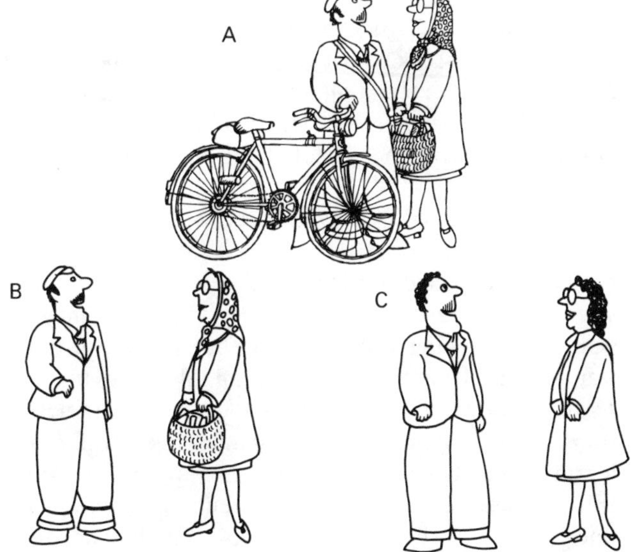

Figure 23 Tracing for reuse
(A) *(Original textbook illustration (from R. Musman,* Britain Today *(Longman, 1973), p. 12).*
(B) *Characters traced on to two separate pieces of acetate.*
(C) *A few small changes to make the figures even more reusable.*

(a) When tracing, ignore the background. Draw only the figures themselves. Try to leave out any features which are not essential for recognizing the character.

(b) If two figures overlap, draw them on to separate pieces of acetate. Then they can be used together or apart, facing each other, or with their backs to each other. You will have to supply some missing lines yourself.

(c) If you are very bold, you can make a few minor changes as you trace. These changes will allow you to use the characters in a wider range of situations.

(d) For details of how such figures can be used, including guidance on suitable sizes, etc., see Chapter 11.

4.3 ALTERING THE SIZE OF A PICTURE

It is worth looking for a figure to copy which is of roughly the same size as your general stock of overhead projector characters. I find a convenient height for standing figures to be between 5 and 7 cm. If a figure is too big or too small, try to alter it to the right scale by one of the following methods (after Harrison, 1978).

(a) *Project* the original (via overhead projector or episcope) on to a sheet of paper pinned to a nearby wall. Adjust the projection distance until the image on the wall is the same size as your intended transparency. Trace this image on the wall. Your tracing will be shaky, but when you trace your transparency from the paper you can tidy things up.

(b) *Draw squares* on the original (or place a suitable squared transparency – bought or home-made – over it). Draw or find a grid of larger (or smaller) squares to put under your blank transparency. Then copy the contents of each square from one grid to the other, as in Figure 24. With line drawings, this is quite a quick process. If the picture is complex, simplify the original by drawing over its outline in a medium-thick pen before copying it to the required scale.

(c) *Pantographs* like the one in Figure 25 are sold in many toyshops. They are useful for enlarging only. The anchor point must be steady: in the best designs, the anchor point is attached to the working surface. Enlarge first in pencil, using the pantograph. Then trace neatly in free-hand on to a transparency.

Figure 24 Enlarging
(From 'Enlarging small pictures' by K. M. Harrison, 1978).

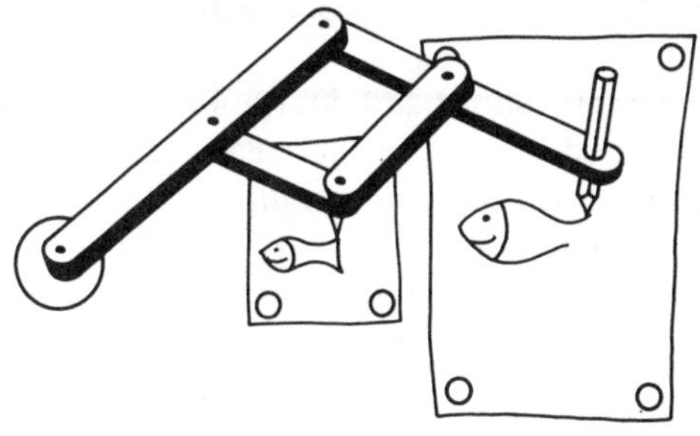

Figure 25 Pantograph

4.4 STOCK CHARACTERS

What about making your own pictures? It is worth a try, even if you are quite sure that you cannot draw.

I am not, myself, enamoured of pinmen. They are all very well for skinny action (*he's running, digging, or climbing,* and this is no doubt what keeps him so thin). But they have no charm, to my mind. And they are not very useful for expressing character or mood. Even on the blackboard, my experience is that I need static figures more often than active ones. On the overhead projector, as we shall see, there are other ways of showing action.

Bellmen are a cheerful alternative to pinmen (see Figure 26). The shape is equally simple to draw. Feet are often unnecessary, but can easily be added to indicate the direction of movement. Hands and feet are easy to draw if the shapes are kept very simple, as in Figure 27. These figures work equally well on the blackboard.

Figure 26 Pinman and basic bellman

Figure 27 Add hands and feet if necessary

'*Tags*' are added for identity. In Figure 28 the old lady's hair, the rabbit's ears and the policeman's helmet and buttons are examples of tags.

Look out for these shorthand indications of identity. Once someone has invented them, they are easy to assimilate into your own drawing. Any illustrator who *simplifies* and *joins up his lines* is a good model for overhead projector (or blackboard) work. Dick Bruna would be ideal (indeed, the rabbit in Figure 28 owes a great deal to him). Edward Ardizzone or Quentin Blake (see Figure 22 for an example of the latter's pleasant line) are too quirky and delicate to serve as models for our stock of classroom cues and stereotypes.

Figure 28 'Tags' add character and identity

Note the *stages* of simplification illustrated in Figure 29. Start your sketch with a basic bellman: round head and bell-shaped body. Add tags to your sketch. Then trace the transparency in a thicker pen to force yourself to simplify and tidy things up further.

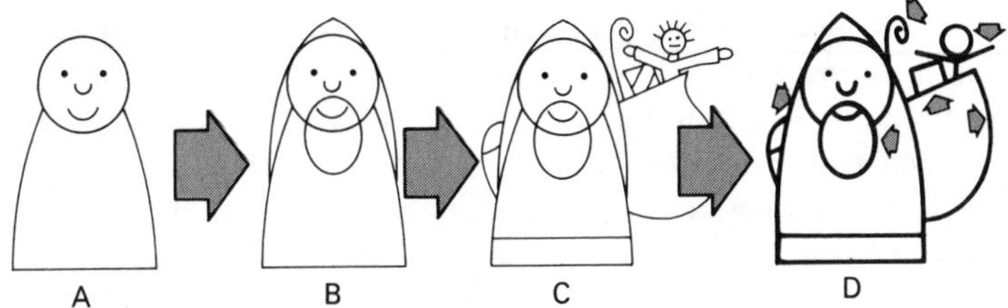

Figure 29 Drawing for projection
(A) *Start with basic bellman on ordinary white paper. Make him about 6 cm high.*
(B) *Add 'tags' for identity.*
(C) *Elaborate if you are enjoying yourself.*
(D) *Place an acetate over the drawing. Copy in a thicker pen. This will force you to simplify and tidy up (see arrowed points). Remember: only bold lines project well.*

Bellmen are obligingly adaptable, as Figure 30 shows. Try out a few of your own, or trace some suitable textbook characters, and see how effectively they can be combined on the overhead projector. They only need to be bold and simple.

Figure 30 Bellmen can do anything

If you do have an irrational fear of drawing, I do not expect to be able to overcome the problem in a few pages of exhortation. But here is one general hint. For most of us the process of making a new picture is a long one. It involves a great deal of trial and error. Most people stop far too soon in the process of working towards the picture they want. The answer is to continue making sketches of what you want to draw, until you have an approximation of what you are after. Check that it is big enough to project clearly. Then trace your drawing, firmly and confidently, on to the transparency.

It is this final stage which gives polish to the drawing. If the figure is a variation on a stock character you have learnt to draw in all kinds of situations, the polish comes much more easily. Bellmen, or even pinmen, are a good scaffolding on which to construct pictures of your own.

Making and Using Visuals

5 Sheet transparencies

Chapters 6 to 13 are about the addition, removal and movement of bits of the projected image. Sheet transparencies, on the other hand, are static, and cover all or most of the projection area.

The size of the projection area depends on the projector itself and the sightlines in the individual classroom, as we have seen. But let us for convenience reckon on a standard area of 20 × 25 cm, the standard size for the hole in an overhead projector mount. All the stock sizes of acetate and cellofilm can be taped into mounts of this size.

Sheet transparencies can be stored in these mounts or in glassine envelopes (see page 24), or, if they are made of acetate, they can simply be punched and filed with interleaves (see page 24). Here are some uses for sheet transparencies.

5.1 SHORT TEXTS: DICTATIONS, SONGS ETC.

Put a short *dialogue* on to a transparency. Use a different coloured ink for each speaker. It helps to draw pictures of the speakers, in the same colours as their words, to aid identification (see Figure 31). It is often very difficult for beginners to distinguish two speakers on a tape if they are of the same sex.

Alternatively, use colour for emphasis, to draw attention to difficult vocabulary, tonic syllables, key words, or whatever.

For work with the *whole class*, you now have much greater control over your students' attention than if they were using individual books. Even if the students will be working at their own individual speeds later in the lesson, it is often a help to have this control at the stage when the text is first presented. Instructions like *Look at the shorter of the two dialogues on page so-and-so*, or *Close your books now – no peeping*, are made unnecessary. Instructions like *Read the green part*, or *What does this word mean?* are made clearer than their equivalents for the textbook.

Figure 31 Two-colour transparency to illustrate taped dialogue

Charlie Pratt has lost his hat
and Number (6) has found it

Who me (Mr Jones)

Yes You Number (6)

Not me (Mr Jones)

Figure 32 Transparency to cue intonation
*(Part of the script for a game (*Mr Roy's Watch, *or* The Prince of Wales's Hat*) to practise the intonation of surprised questions and short assertions with intermediate classes of children (based on Lee, 1979, pp. 80–1).*

While you are giving a *dictation*, write out the passage on a transparency, or get one of the class to write out his answer on cellofilm instead of ordinary paper. The rest of the class then either check each other's answers against your transparency, or correct the student's projected answer. This is obviously a great time-saver.

Anything that takes *time* to write out, because of colour or other conventions such as the intonation in Figure 32, can be prepared beforehand on a transparency, and then reused indefinitely. Write clearly with a medium thickness overhead projector pen, using the guidelines in Figure 19 above. Lower-case letters (i.e. not all capitals) are recommended; print them for maximum clarity.

Above all, keep overhead projector texts *short*: fifty words is a reasonable *maximum* for a transparency in a foreign language. For longer texts, use a handout.

Use the overhead projector to *dramatize* the presentation of texts. For example, in the game 'Telepathy' (Wright, Betteridge and Buckby, 1979), four short texts are shown. One student (the 'medium') concentrates on one of the texts. The rest of the class write out the text they think the 'medium' has chosen. They do this either from memory, or while looking at the four texts: they must be very short. If you use the overhead projector, you can switch it off before or after the class have written out their guesses. Then, while it is off, get the medium to point to his chosen text, and switch on again. The medium's hand is dramatically silhouetted. Not for nothing was the first overhead projector named 'Belshazzar' (Leggat, 1972)!

5.2 MAPS, DIAGRAMS AND DETAILED PICTURES

There are various very attractive commercially produced maps and diagrams available on transparencies. In a school, you might find that the geography and maths departments have some worth borrowing for language lessons. But the overhead projector encourages you to make your own, and to tailor them to your own purposes. For example, Moorwood (1978) gives examples of diagrams without captions. These require imagination, and explanation involving specific areas of language, to make them make sense.

Suppose you wanted your pupils to practise comparative forms in an appropriate setting. You project the graph in Figure 33 and ask the class to suggest what it might represent (e.g. car production in different companies). Even a free discussion would then be expected to result in a crop of comparative forms.

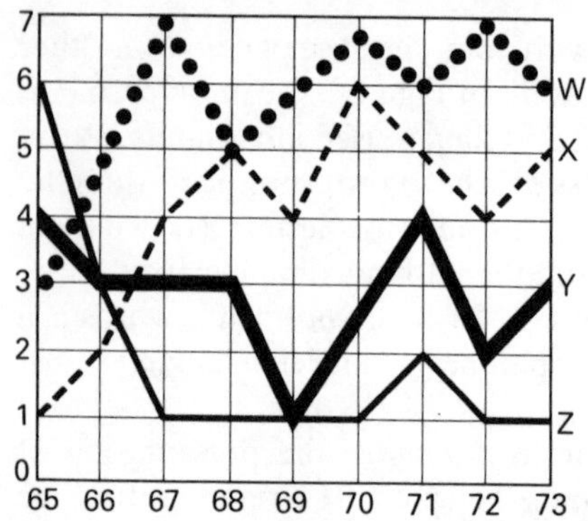

The teacher then asks the students to tell him as much as they can about the graph. The following are some of the sentences that students in an intermediate class produced:

In 1965 Z produced:

- twice as many cars as W.
- more cars than Y.
- far more cars than X.

Figure 33 Unlabelled graph: pupils supply labels
(From Helen Moorwood, Selections from Modern English Teacher *(Longman, 1978), p. 34.)*

Some other suggestions from Moorwood's article are illustrated in Figures 34 to 36. These are all pictures which need care and thought and preparation. They are therefore worth preserving for reuse.

Names, symbols, etc. can be added to the pictures during projection, as the class make their decisions. This can be done in a number of ways already mentioned, without dirtying the original picture, which we want to preserve for reuse. The acetate roll (see page 26), a glassine envelope (see page 24) or an overlay (Chapter 7) could be used.

A cunning alternative is to draw the picture *in reverse* on one side of a transparency, and then to project it *ink side down*. Additions can then be made on the upper side, and washed off later. Pictures like Figures 34 to 36, which involve no writing, can easily be drawn 'backwards'. The only problem is that you have to be a very cool customer to remember which side your transparency is, so to speak, buttered. The main thing is to preserve the original picture for reuse, whatever technique you use.

Pictures such as Figure 34 can obviously be used for other activities, too. A treasure hunt is one possibility. Another would be the presentation stage of N. F. Davies' role play, 'The Island' (Davies, 1980).

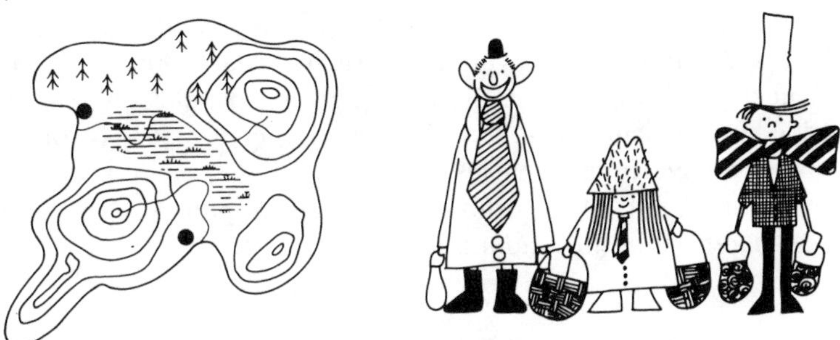

Figure 34 Unlabelled map: pupils provide labels
(Based on Moorwood's suggestion: prepositions of movement and direction are practised while planning the route of a new road. Moorwood, 1978, p. 34.)

Figure 35 Comparative and superlative
(Based on Moorwood's suggestion: 'Three men or women of different heights, sizes, weights and with different length hair, coats, skirts; with different sized bags, umbrellas, etc. – comparative and superlative, "quite" and "very".' Moorwood, 1978, p. 34.)

Figure 36 School timetable
Times, days, lessons can be filled in during lesson. Practise 'have', present simple, expressions of frequency. (Based on description in Moorwood, 1978, p. 34.)

5.2.1. TOWN PLANS

Street maps are even more useful: how many have you drawn in your teaching career? Save yourself some trouble. For most purposes, it is sufficient to make a reusable grid of streets as in Figure 37. For variety, you can turn it through 90° or 180° or project it ink side down. Buildings, rivers, people, etc. can be added for particular lessons, either by drawing or writing on one of the protective transparencies mentioned above, or by keeping a small stock of little silhouettes (see Chapter 9), or mini-transparencies in slide mounts (see Chapter 10).

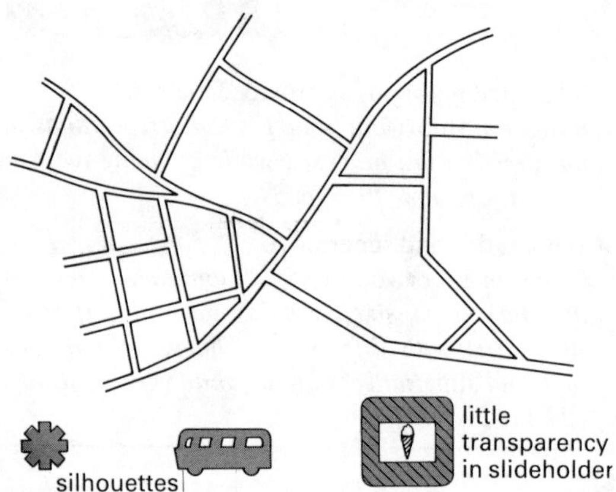

Figure 37 Reusable street grid

In Figure 37, for example, Student A places the silhouette star on the street plan and announces, 'I'm here.' Student B then *imagines* where the ice-cream shop stands. B then gives A oral instructions on how to get to the ice-cream shop by bus. A moves the bus across the illuminated transparency. When he reaches the right spot, B gives him the ice-cream symbol to put on the grid.

You can continue to build up the map in this way. Alternatively, the ice-cream symbol can be put in place beforehand and Student A, blindfolded, can steer his bus there on instructions shouted by the whole class. (There is the advantage that 'left' and 'right' are the same for Student A as for the rest of the class, even though he is facing them.)

See 'West Winghythe' (Elgar and Rees, 1978) for fuller development of a flannelboard village of the same type, which would work very well on the overhead projector. You will no doubt think of alternative versions for classes of older students.

5.2.2 CHECKLISTS

More realistic and specific sheet transparencies can be devised. Here is an idea for any ESP class where pupils have to learn *check routines* in English (Burkart, 1980). For example, airline pilots have to go through these routines before take-off. Mechanics learn to use new machines through similar workshop routines.

First you make a transparency from a photograph or diagram of a cockpit or workshop layout. The labelling is printed separately, on an overlay (see Chapter 7 for ways of doing this). You then read out the relevant checklist for pronunciation. Then you 'perform' the routines on the transparency, touching the various labelled controls as you come to them in the checklist.

New vocabulary is then explained. The checklist is repeated chorally while the teacher again simulates the routines. Then one student simulates the routines while another reads out the checklist, eventually without the labelling.

Burkart includes checklists for simple classroom objects to introduce the conventions. For example, *Insert pencil into sharpener. Pencil inserted. Apply slight inward pressure. Pressure applied,* etc. These routines provide amusing practice in the devising of explicit instructions. They could be used with non-specialist classes.

5.2.3 'BUSY' PICTURES

A detailed, bustling picture, preferably drawn in black and white so that it can be photocopied clearly, can be used on a sheet transparency. The important thing is to remember that such pictures are difficult to assimilate. The first method below exploits this difficulty by asking pupils to remember as much as they can of a scene. The second method avoids the difficulty by concentrating on individual elements of the picture.

Any 'witness' game (e.g. Wright *et al.*, 1979) can be tried with detailed pictures. First tell the class you are going to test their reliability as witnesses. Then project the picture for a limited time. After switching off, ask questions (eliciting responses in past tenses, especially the past continuous). *You* still have the transparency in front of you as an *aide-mémoire*, but do not peer at it too obviously, or you will get the tenses confused. (What is a *past* picture for the class should not be a *present* picture for you.)

A technique for using a detailed picture with less able pupils is described by Langer (1972). A monochrome transparency of a picture is projected. To focus attention on individual elements in the picture, you trace those items in colour, or circle them with a water-based colour pen. This simplifies comprehension of the picture. It is actually an *advantage* here to have a rather faint transparency to start with: the coloured sections then stand out all the better.

5.3 BACKDROPS

Figure 37 introduced the idea of a sheet transparency as a *backdrop*, i.e. a setting for the movement of smaller figures (silhouettes, mini-transparencies, etc.) The making of these is described in later chapters.

The most abstract type of backdrop would be one sheet of *colour*, e.g. a red theatre gel representing 'the desert'. Self-adhesive colour sheets can be combined to imitate those magnet-boards which are half green and half blue. 'Blue up' equals sky; 'blue down' equals sea. But in all these cases the backdrop colour should be *very* light, and the smaller figures should be drawn in black or dark blue lines. Otherwise they will not show up clearly.

If the class complain of *glare* from the overhead projector image, this can be reduced by using a very light orange theatre gel in a mount, as a permanent backdrop to your transparencies. If it is only you, the operator, who is complaining of glare, this must be coming from the projection stage itself, not from the projected image. In this case you can buy a little screen in smoked plastic to attach to the lens assembly. This cuts down the glare which reaches your eyes. One is shown in Figure 6.

Another useful backdrop using colour is illustrated in Figure 38. It is made up of strips of light shades of the common colours. Outline figures on separate pieces of acetate can then be rapidly manipulated on this backdrop for colour practice: *What's this? It's a red dog. What colour is the fish? It's blue*, etc. The colour backdrop in Figure 38, used with three line drawings, provides cues for fifteen adjective–noun combinations. In other words, it replaces fifteen flashcards. Some of the combinations may be rather arbitrary (*green pig, blue cow,* etc.) but this should not matter when the structure is first being presented and practised.

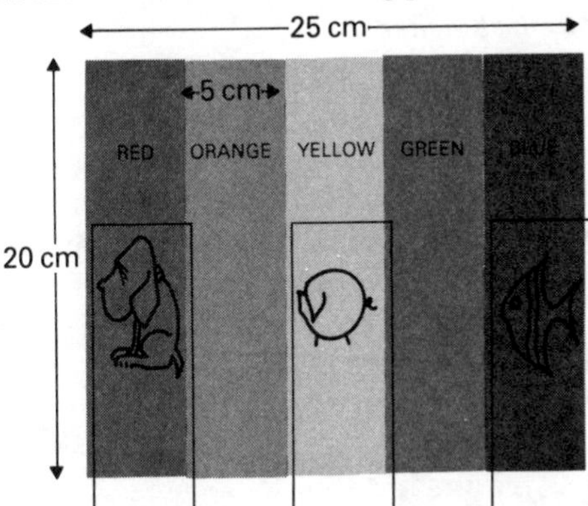

Figure 38 Colour strips

Figure 39 Backdrop of house interior

Line drawings like Figure 37 can be used repeatedly. Useful stock subjects are: a house interior (Figure 39), a shop interior (just the shelves, weighing scales and cash register: the goods can be added according to topic), the High Street (identifying individual shops), or a plan of an individual room in a house. These can be peopled with silhouettes or transparent characters traced from the textbook in order to practise directions, prepositions of place, etc., or simply to provide a visual context for the dramatisation of a text or situation:

How do I get to the butcher's?
He's going upstairs.
Have you any cheese?

Photocopied transparencies give realism where necessary. If you have backdrops of the Houses of Parliament, the surface of the moon, Shakespeare's Globe Theatre, or the San Francisco earthquake (to pick a few possibilities at random), the classroom walls are not going to limit your range of movement.

Figure 40 Photocopy of interior

A photocopied diagram such as Figure 40 might save you drawing a whole house. For use as a backdrop, it is important that there should be no large black areas which would conceal superimposed characters. The rug in Figure 40 would be a nuisance, for instance. There are two ways round this. One is to cut dark areas out of the original, replacing them by outlines. The other is to use a heat copy paper which would reproduce the black original as a translucent coloured area which would conceal nothing (see page 29).

5.4 SUMMARY

A sheet transparency does not take long to make. It is worth storing for reuse if you choose the items carefully. If it is to be used as a backdrop for other transparencies, it should be light, so that it neither obscures details, nor cuts the overall brightness to an unacceptable level.

It does not matter if the scale of the backdrop is smaller than that of the foreground figures: it is acceptable that the 'background' be smaller in scale than the 'foreground'. Indeed, this is the only way one could indicate perspective on the overhead projector.

If you mount a backdrop transparency, tape it to the *upper* side of the mount, so that you have a smooth surface on which to move the other items about. Otherwise they will snag on the edges of the mount. (This method of mounting is a good habit to get into, as *any* sheet transparency might conceivably at some stage be used as a backdrop for a smaller item.)

6 *Writing during Projection*

It will already be clear that my strategy is to prepare as much material as possible before projection. This gives one time to plan a transparency that will be clear, attractive and sufficiently general in application to be worth reusing, whereas writing on the overhead projector during projection results in sketchy work which is going to have to be erased anyway. It is partly a matter of taste and teaching style, but it seems to me that for ephemera one might as well use the blackboard.

Another reason for keeping additions *in situ* to a minimum is that some projectors get hot and your pens dry up while you are trying to write on the hot plate.

However, there are cases where *additions* to previously prepared transparencies can be made during the course of a lesson. The addition may depend on *choices* which the students themselves will be making. The blank graph in Figure 33 would have been labelled in this way. On the other hand, it may be the actual *process* of making the addition that one wishes to dramatize. Filling in the form illustrated in Figure 18 would be an example of this.

Additions to transparencies require the protection of the original image in one of the ways described for sheet transparencies in Chapter 5:

(a) Place the transparency under the acetate roll and make additions on the latter.
(b) Store the transparency in a glassine envelope and make additions on that during projection.
(c) Use a separate sheet of acetate or cellofilm as an overlay for additions.

(d) Project the original image ink side down, so that you can make additions on the clean upper surface.

In short, additions are best made on a different surface from the original, even if the second surface is the *back* of the original transparency.

Some practitioners apparently leave gaps in spirit-based transparencies and then add water-based bits *in situ*. I have never had any success with this. If the transparency is on acetate, water-based additions tend to dry up and disappear while I am writing them. On cellofilm, removal of the addition tends to wrinkle the whole transparency.

Given these restrictions, here are some examples of additions usefully made during projection.

Some games require a *grid* which has to be redrawn each time you play the game. Some of these grids are very simple. For instance, 'Pattern Puzzle' (Lee, 1979) always requires five circles, which are filled with different letters each time the game is played. Drawing five circles is not very taxing, but if the game is popular, it might be worth making a more ornate version of this grid (see Figure 41). The new letters are then drawn *in situ* each time the game is played.

Figure 41 Decorative grid for 'Pattern Puzzle'

The idea of the game is that groups have to write down as many words as possible in a given time, all of which must contain the letter in the middle circle ('E' in the example) and some or all of the other letters.

Many of the crossword games in Lee's book can be played by the whole class using either a pre-drawn grid on the overhead projector, or a blackboard with painted grid lines (for maths). But games like Scrabble can be equipped with the more sophisticated grids they require (triple word scores, etc.). This is best done on the overhead projector if the whole class is to play. The words are then written in as *in situ* additions for each game.

If your class is frequently divided into competing groups for games, you could make a reusable *scoring grid* (see Figure 42), and write in the scores each time you use it. (Alternative scoring systems are described in Chapter 8.)

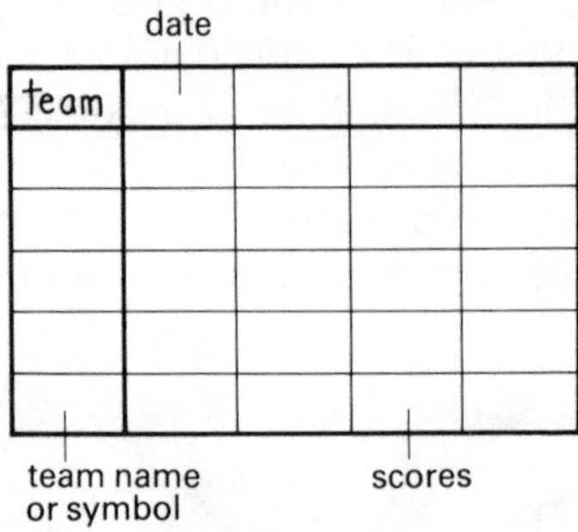

Figure 42 Scoring grid for class games

Transparencies of *texts* can be added to *in situ*, either by the teacher (drawing attention to key points, etc.) or by a student (marking stressed syllables while listening to a tape of a text, etc.) Such graphically simple additions can also be made with silhouetted markers (matches for underlining, drawing pins for dots, etc.) or with colour circles in non-adhesive plastic.

Examples where the actual *process* is of interest include *Guess what I'm drawing* games, to practise *Is it a —? It can't/must be a —*, etc., as in Figure 43. Normally these would best be done on the blackboard, but if the first part of the drawing is to be prepared beforehand, the overhead projector might be quicker.

Figure 43 Guess what I'm drawing

The same is true of 'joining the dots' pictures, which take time to prepare, if the whole class is to do them together. 'Joining the dots' can be fun, not only with beginners who may concurrently be finding their way about the number system in their own language, but with more sophisticated 'clues' for older learners, such as the offering in Figure 44.

.V .P .F .W

.C .H .O .N

.J .Y .M .R

.I .X .D .S

.A .G .Q .U

.E .L .T .B

Figure 44 'Join the dots' for older classes
Procedure: Make questions (hard or easy), e.g. 'This one's chocolate; the — one's vanilla: what's the missing word? *(Answer:* other.) *Use the initial letters of the answers in your grid. Here, for example, 16 answers might give the initial letters* O–H–P–F–O–R–S–U–B–T–L–E–A–I–D–S ('OHP for subtle aids'). *Join those letters with straight lines to reveal the hidden picture. Other letters in the grid are dummies: the grid itself gives no clue to what the eventual picture might be.*

A *marking system* needs visual explanation, and it helps the student to see what the teacher actually *does* which results in all that red ink. A transparency of student work, such as the example in Figure 20 above, can be projected, and 'marked' *in situ* with a red projector pen.

Visual explanation would be particularly necessary with a complex marking system such as Sivell's 'three-pencil method' (1980). This requires student work to be written out in three different colours: blue for the first draft, pupils' own corrections in black, and the pupils' own final corrections, referring to a list of frequent errors provided by the teacher, in red. (The idea is to get students to commit a free first draft to paper, and then to train them in self-correction of that first draft.) The system would be conveniently shown in action on the overhead projector.

Any marking system which used conventional signs which might be unfamiliar to the students would need illustrated explanation in the same way. The overhead projector would allow you to keep the illustration for use with the next class.

In summary, the basic principles of writing during projection are:

(a) Add sparingly.
(b) Protect the original while doing so.

7 *Overlays*

In a general sense, any transparency which is superimposed on another is an 'overlay', but the term is usually reserved for additions to the base transparency which are *integral* to it, and which would therefore probably be meaningless if they were projected on their own. Thus, for example, in Figure 45, where the words on the overlay are only meaningful when they are superimposed on the base.

If the overlay and base can only be used together, it is obviously a good idea to *attach* the one to the other, in such a way that they *register* (the overlay always falls into place). This is done by *hinging*, either by taping the overlay to one edge of the base transparency as in Figure 45 or, more robustly, by mounting the base and then taping the overlay to one edge of the mount.

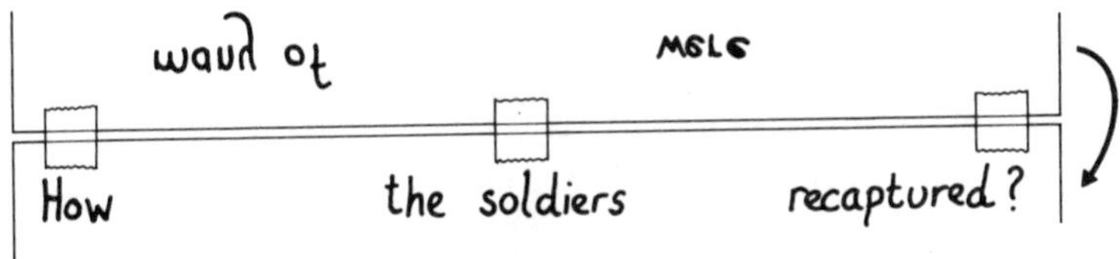

Figure 45 Hinging of overlay to base
'How (many of) the soldiers (were) recaptured?'

A commercial hinging system such as Flipatran (see Figure 17 above) does the same job.

Note that if you want two transparencies to register, but to be separate, you can tape them into individual mounts, which will then fall into register on the pins which most overhead projectors have at the edge of the glass plate for this purpose. If both transparencies had their own independent uses, this would be a good method.

Obvious uses for overlays in language teaching include any kind of gapped text. A *cloze* test, for instance, with words removed and later revealed on the overlay as in Figure 46.

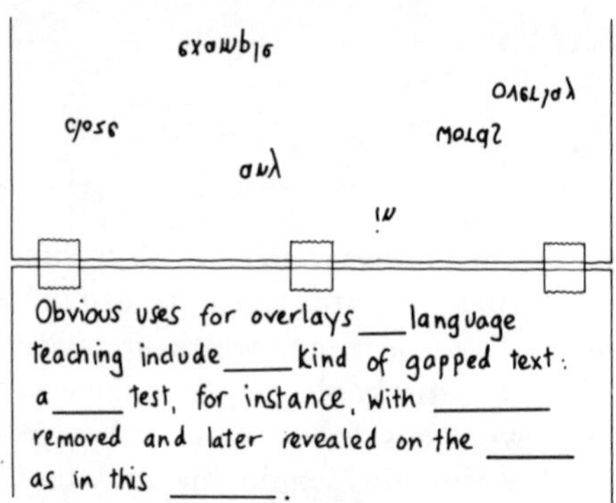

Figure 46 Cloze test: missing words on overlay

A *'disappearing dialogue'* can be presented in full and then the overlay can be removed, leaving only key words as an *aide mémoire* (see Figure 47).

In the same way, a *substitution table* can be projected complete, so that students can read sentences off it in the presentation phase. The overlay can then be turned back, leaving the invariant parts of the structure, from which the class can make their own sentences in the practice phase (see Figure 48).

Texts with overlays are made as follows:

(a) Rough out the complete text on ordinary paper, using an underlay to guide you (see Figure 19).
(b) Circle the words which will appear on the overlay (i.e. which will disappear from the image at some stage).
(c) Place a transparency over the rough draft and neatly trace only those words which are *not* circled.
(d) Keeping that transparency in place, fit a second transparency exactly over it and trace only the circled words, making sure they fit the gaps in the base transparency.
(e) Tape the two transparencies together along one side, so that the overlay is hinged freely.

S: Industrial Cleaning: can I help you?
R.W: ___, my name's Whitney.
S: ___ ___es, Mr Whitney.
Mrs Marsh was expecting you to call.
___ ___ ___ through.
C.M: ___ ___ here.
R.W: ___ ___, Richard here.

Figure 47 Disappearing dialogue
Key words on base transparency: remainder of dialogue on overlay.

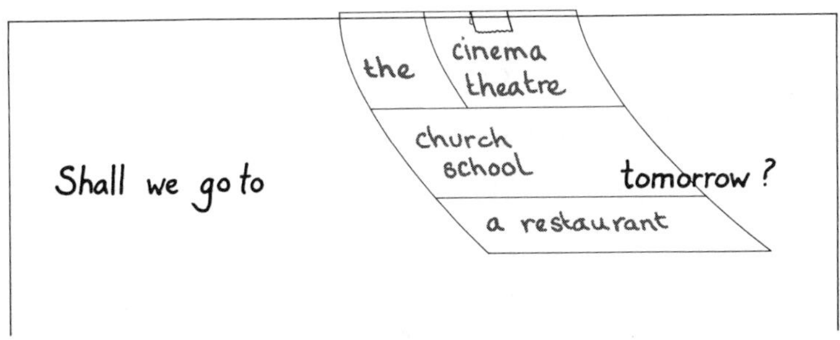

Figure 48 Substitution table
Invariable parts of drill sentence on base transparency: variable parts on overlay.

You can have more than one overlay attached to a base. But if all the overlays are hinged to the same side, as in Figure 49 (a), you can only use them in order and cumulatively.

One alternative is to hinge one overlay to each side of the base transparency as in Figure 49 (b). The maximum number of overlays by this system is obviously four, and you need to be a bit of a juggler to operate them. Tape each overlay well back from the inside edge of the mount. This will leave room for the other overlays to overlap the edge of the mount without getting mixed up in your hinging tape. A good system with two or three overlays which you want to be free to use in any order.

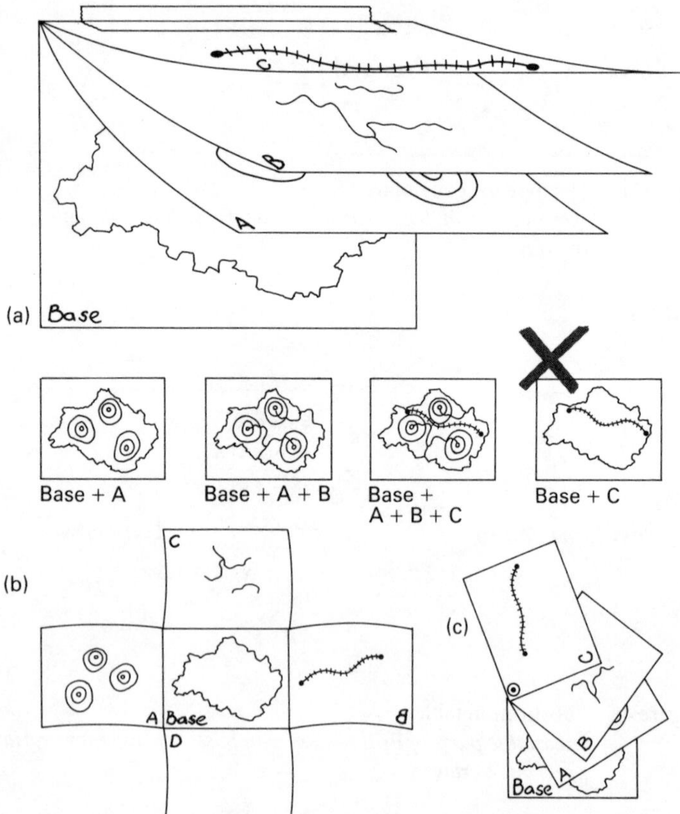

Figure 49 Multiple overlays

Another alternative is to *grummet* all the overlays to one corner as in Figure 49 (c). A grummet is a metal eyelet which holds all the transparencies together, but allows them to rotate independently about the eyelet. A paper fastener through punched holes would serve the same purpose. This method means that you have to swing each overlay into position to register on the base transparency. With a complex diagram it is therefore advisable to make a registration mark in the corner of the base transparency and each overlay. The advantage is that you can combine a lot of overlays and use them in any order.

Overlay techniques are often used for maps: an outline appears on the base and there are overlays of relief, drainage, communications, etc. Diagrams of machinery may have separate overlays of, for example, the electrical and hydraulic systems.

Overlays are fun to make, but difficult to store. The method is only necessary if registration of the separate elements is crucial. Taping one item to another means that you lose a certain amount of flexibility. In the example of the tree, for instance (see Figure 3), if the apple and leaf transparencies were grummeted or taped to the base you would not be able to slide them about to illustrate: *The apples/leaves are falling/have fallen off the tree,* although you would still be able to elicit: *It's summer/The tree loses its leaves every winter/There are going to be a lot of apples*/and so on.

8 *Masking and Revelation*

The simplest mask is an ordinary sheet of paper. You can slide this around on top of a transparency, blocking off various sections of the projected image. You may even wish to mask the *whole* image instead of turning the projector on and off intermittently. If the paper is thin, the operator can see the transparency *through* the mask, but for the audience the projected image is blocked completely.

The main thing with masks is not to fiddle about with them. They should be moved confidently and as little as possible during projection. Movement is distracting, especially if it has no apparent purpose. Another distraction is splashes of light around the *edges* of the mask, especially if it is an odd shape (see Figure 50).

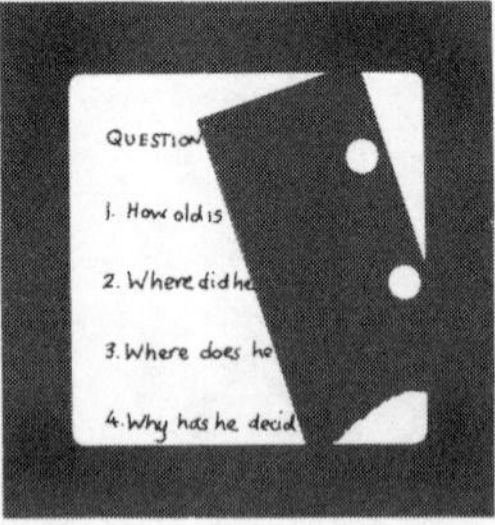

Figure 50 Distracting use of mask

A plain, untorn sheet of paper is the least distracting of masks, as well as the simplest. Some published ideas on masking involve cutting out complex shapes of limited use. It is always worth asking yourself whether the idea would not work just as well with a plain sheet of paper. Often all that is needed is a little redesigning of the transparency beneath.

Published transparencies often have a tendency to present too much information on a single sheet, because they are expensive, and space is at a premium. It often helps to present elements of these transparencies one at a time, masking the remainder with as many sheets of paper as necessary (see Figure 51).

(a) *'What does he/she want for Christmas?'*

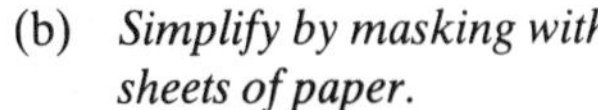

(b) *Simplify by masking with sheets of paper.*

(c) *Or focus attention with patches of non-adhesive colour.*

Figure 51 Crowded multiple image

In Chapters 9 to 11, pictures are built up by adding elements. It is often possible to build up a situation by *revelation* of the *existing* elements. In Figure 52, for instance, the picture has been designed so that a mask can be moved across it in five stages. During the first stage the mask is at 'B' and only A–B is visible. You ask questions about Alfonso, including, *What's he doing, do you think? (Carrying something?) Right.* (Move mask to C.) *What's he carrying?* And so on.

Figure 52 Revelation of picture in stages

The key points are: Alfonso cannot carry all three pineapples over the bridge at the same time because they would be too heavy. Nor can he throw them, because they would be damaged. Nor can he leave one behind, because the bears would eat it. Reveal the whole picture before asking how Alfonso will get across the river. The story, but not the picture, is from *English Teaching Forum,* vol. 18, no. 3 (1980), and you will find Alfonso's solution under that reference in the present volume.

The technique of gradually revealing items of information will work with many pictures that are not designed with that technique in mind, but you may need two or three bits of paper for masking, and you may have to juggle a bit.

Separate pictures in a *cartoon strip* can be revealed in the same way, and not necessarily in chronological order: starting with the

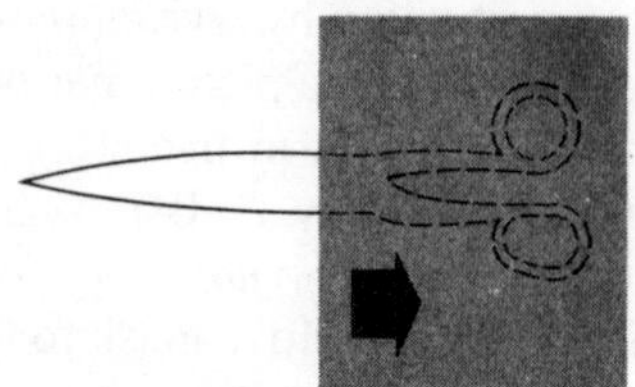

Figure 53 Gradual revelation of object

last picture should produce some speculations in the present perfect.

A single picture or object can be gradually revealed in a guessing game (see Figure 53). An alternative to masking is to project the object *out of focus* to get people guessing, either by altering the focus on the projector, or by holding the object off the glass plate, hiding it from the direct view of the audience by holding a piece of paper between it and them. Andrew Wright is keen on this technique, and his excellent series of articles with J. Y. K. Kerr in *Modern English Teacher* are required reading for anyone who wants some inspiration on the *lyrical* side of overhead projection! (See Kerr, 1978a, 1978b and Wright, 1979a, 1979b.)

Texts can be revealed line by line, to control when, and for how long, each line is read. For instance: write on a transparency a set of comprehension questions about a taped passage. Reveal the first question only, and start the tape. As soon as a student puts up his hand to answer, stop the tape. If the answer is correct, reveal the next question and play more tape. (The method works equally well with written exercises.)

Reading for content can be encouraged by showing a text for a short time, and then switching off while questions are asked on the content. With longer texts, the pace can be controlled by showing a sentence at a time, with the use of a mask.

A set of *homework* answers could be gone through efficiently by writing out questions and correct answers on alternate lines and revealing them one by one. Alternatively, the questions (or other cues) could be written in one column, if they are short. The responses could be revealed one by one in the other column (see Figure 54). This method works well with chaining drills, such as the one illustrated in Figure 54.

Figure 54 Gradual revelation of drill

The main points of a *lecture* can be written out on a single transparency and revealed one by one as they come up. This results in the kind of perfect visual summary that the model blackboard-user is supposed to produce. From the lecturer's point of view, too, having committed oneself to acetate is a very good way of ensuring that one talks about what one had planned to talk about.

What has been said about gradual revelation applies equally well to gradual *concealment*. If a song is to be memorized, for instance, the words can be gradually concealed by masking, until the class are singing with no visual cue.

A substitution table, like the one in Figure 48, could easily be masked instead of being overlaid, just leaving *Shall we go to . . .* as the cue.

Even a cloze passage like the one in Figure 46 could be replaced by a single transparency, if one had a lot of little objects, such as erasers, with which to mask individual words. It all depends on which method you think is more convenient.

Books on materials for the overhead projector often describe complex masks with lots of little doors, like advent calendars. It is difficult to see the point of these. It is a lot of work to make a multiple hinged mask for a transparency. The little doors either leak light round the edges (Figure 55 (a)) or overlap each other so that they have to be used in a set order (Figure 55 (b)). If the mask is to work properly, one therefore has to make each door a little bigger than the hole it covers, as in Figure 55 (c). And after all this, the mask only fits *one* design of transparency!

Bell & Howell (1968) illustrate a multiple hinged mask which they recommend for reuse, but if the doors have to be opened in order from top to bottom, one might as well use a sheet of paper.

There might be some point in making such a mask if the doors can be opened at random as in Figure 55 (c). You could have six windows, and make a transparency which contained, for each window, the title for an impromptu speech. A student in an advanced class could then throw a dice or otherwise decide which of the numbered doors he wanted to open. He would then have to speak for, say, one minute without hesitations, on the revealed topic. A number of television competitions use this method of boxes containing secrets.

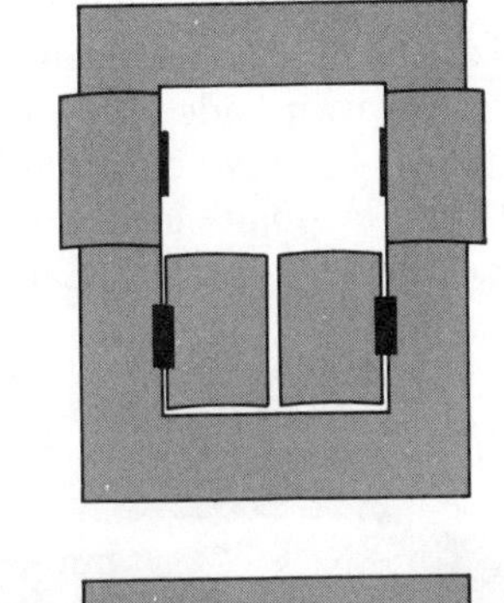

(a) *Cut from one piece. Doors open in any order but leak light at edges.*

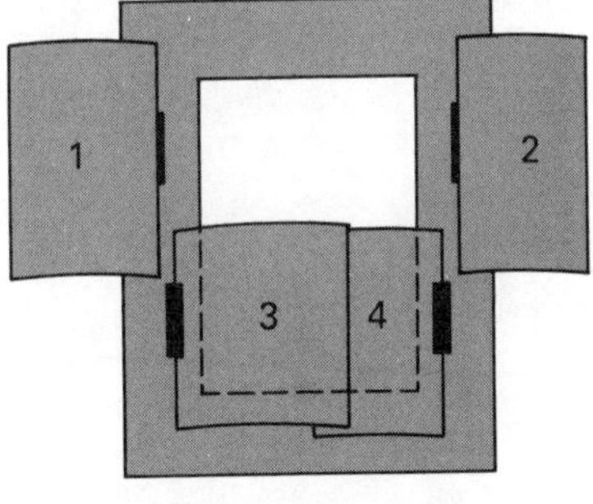

(b) *Overlapping doors. No light leaks but doors must be opened in set order.*

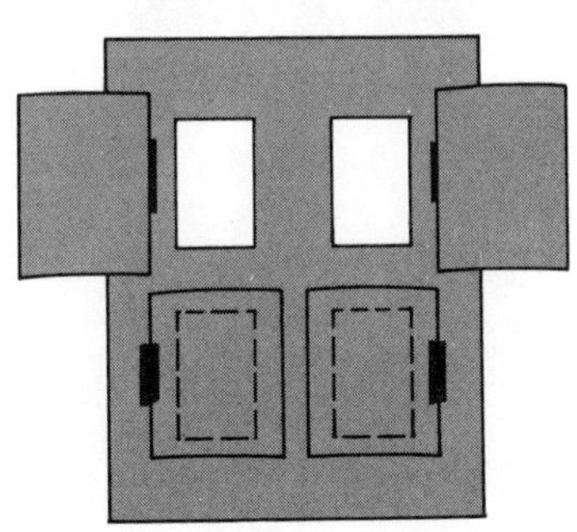

(c) *Separate windows. Doors can open in any order. No light leaks. But window frame may conceal parts of transparency.*

Figure 55 Problems with hinged masks

The criterion in the case of masks is, as it always should be, 'Does it help the audience?' Masks often look impressive on the *projector*, but not on the *screen*, where it matters. Revelation is a very valuable technique, but more often than not you only need a sheet of paper to do it.

Finally, Lee (1979) suggests using symbols in scoring children's games. Each point scored is symbolized by an extra waggon on a train, or an extra example of the team's own badge, or, 'faces getting more cheerful as the line lengthens'. Such symbols could be kept on a transparency and revealed point by point during a game (see Figure 56). You would need a separate mask for each team.

Figure 56 Scoresheet for class games
Team A ('Kawasaki') have four points; Team B ('Honda') have three points. (After Lee, 1979.)

9 *Silhouettes*

Opaque objects with interesting or recognizable outlines are silhouetted dramatically on the overhead projector. They can be smaller than the 6 cm recommended for translucent figures in Chapter 4: cutouts of 3 cm are fine, and even figures 1 cm high will be perfectly clear to the audience if they are designed with care.

Apart from cutouts, you can use *real objects* (buttons, matches, paper clips, etc.) in Kim's Game, which works very well on the overhead projector. A useful language-producing variant is to replace one object by a similar object for the second viewing:

The pencil is shorter.
The toothpaste has been used, etc.

Less obvious objects can be used in various guessing games. It may be necessary to shield the side of the glass plate facing the class so that they can only see the objects in their projected form. For example: *How much money is there on the projector? Anyone who guesses right can have it all.* Objects which are hard to recognize when projected on end (pen, nail, pencil, roll of tape, etc.) or are vague in outline (handkerchief, rosebud, etc.) can be guessed at.

Kerr (1978a, 1978b) and Wright (1979a, 1979b) are the richest sources for ideas on silhouetting. In 'Blobs' (Wright, Betteridge and Buckby, 1979), analogies are practised. Teachers or students arrange torn paper, sand, etc. on the projector and then discuss the projected image:

Beginners: *I can see a —*
It looks like a —
I think it's a —

Advanced: How people's interpretations reflect their personalities.

A very expressive face can be created within a large silhouetted outline (see Figure 57). Broken matches are used for eyebrows, drawing-pins for eyes, an elastic band for a mouth. One use is to give a 'face' to expressive voices heard on tape. The expression is quickly changed from one emotional extreme to another. Another is to make a silhouette with one or two such faces, with 'thought bubbles' above them, such as one sees in strip cartoons. These are excellent for all kinds of dialogues. You put thoughts into the bubbles, and ask the class to supply the dialogue (Kerr, 1978a).

If you can manage not to lose the small bits and pieces used for eyes and other features here, you can use the same bits and pieces for adding comments to a projected text: broken matches for intonation marks, unbroken matches for underlining, erasers to mask individual words, or a drawing-pin moving along a song text as the class sing, as the 'bouncing ball' used to follow the words in the old music hall (Brims, 1978).

What materials should one use for small silhouettes? One possibility is to use a fairly robust material such as cardboard (or balsa wood sheets, or tin, if you can cut it easily). Less permanent shapes can be moulded in plasticine. But these are rather a problem to store. I keep mine in a tobacco tin, or the stamp section of my wallet if I have to carry them around.

A convenient alternative is to mount and file each silhouette on a standard sized 5 × 21 cm acetate strip (see Chapter 11 for filing details). The silhouette itself can then be of paper, preferably self-adhesive, as any glue used to attach the silhouette to the acetate is likely to show up as a smear when projected.

Designing silhouettes requires a little experimentation. Some good pictures can look quite incomprehensible as silhouettes, but good outlines can be most effective (see Figures 58 to 60). Like transparencies, they are reversible, and should be designed with this in mind. Silhouettes can be moved about a transparency very conveniently and effectively. With static pictures, it could take a long time to practise, *She's on the bed. Now she's under the bed. Now she's in the cupboard.* The cat in Figure 58, on a transparency of a bedroom, would demonstrate all these spatial relationships in no time.

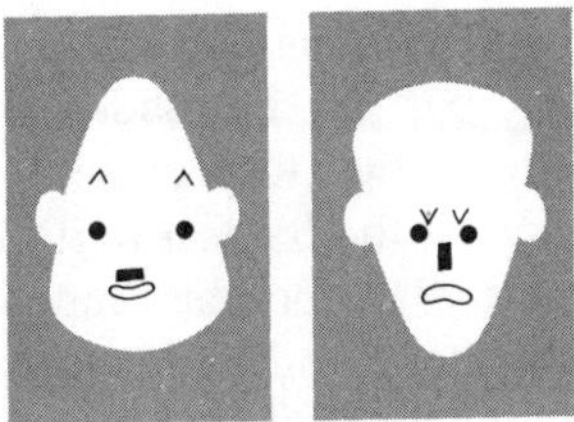

Figure 57 Silhouetted faces: same elements in both pictures

Figure 58 Silhouettes and perspective
When making silhouettes from drawings, avoid perspective effects, as these look peculiar when projected.

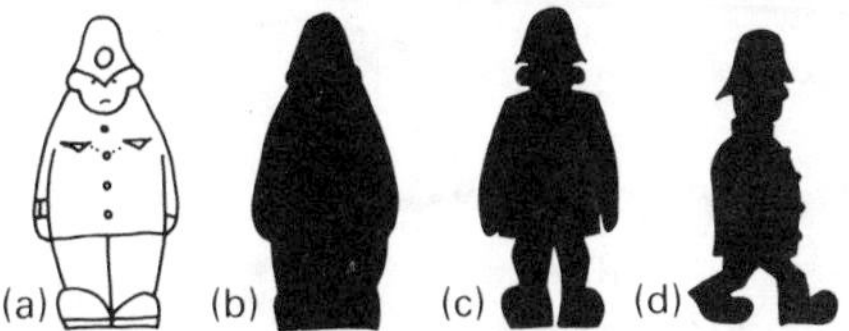

Figure 59 Adjusting silhouettes
Some figures (a) *have uninformative silhouettes* (b) *and will need to be adjusted* (c) *or redrawn completely* (d).

Figure 60 Sherlock Holmes
Use self-adhesive paper with backing attached. First use file punch to make centre of magnifying glass. Then draw rest of silhouette and cut out. Remove backing paper and mount on acetate strip. Add bow on hat with black spirit-based projector pen.

Technical diagrams often benefit from a silhouetted movable element. In Figure 61, part of a rubber band is attached to a transparency of the vocal tract to represent the tongue. This is used to plot the position of the highest part of the tongue for the various cardinal vowels. The points cannot be plotted on an overlay because the rubber band makes this inconvenient. The transparency would probably be drawn in reverse, therefore, and projected ink side down, as explained in Chapter 5. The rubber band is then attached to the upper side of the transparency, where the points can be plotted, and later erased, without damage to the original transparency.

In a course for doctors (McRae, 1975), a sketch of a fractured

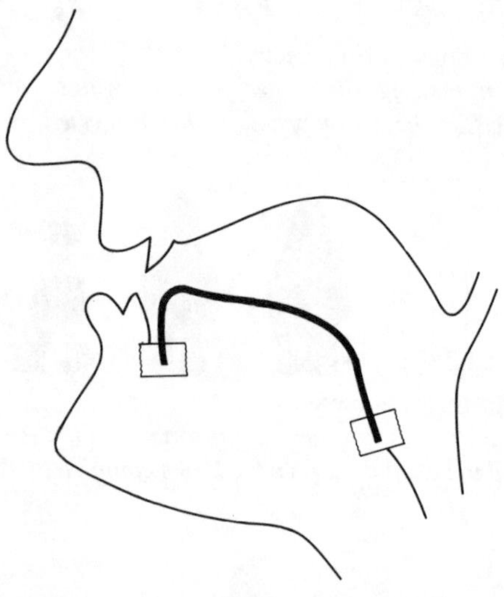

Figure 61 Transparency of vocal tract for plotting tongue positions: rubber band for tongue
Tongue utilizes natural bend in rubber band. Anchored with tape or glue.

femoral neck was used as the base transparency. A (real) Smith-Patersen nail was silhouetted on this to show how it would be positioned. Other topics that would be dramatically illustrated by simple silhouette symbols would be: navigation, traffic movement, conveyor flow, chess, etc. (See also Powell, 1964.)

Figure 57 consisted of what might be called a *sheet silhouette*, to distinguish it from the small, movable silhouettes I have just been describing. The outline of the head concentrates attention on the illuminated area much more than a line would do. Wright (1979a) suggests projecting a sheet silhouette of a keyhole, simply to get pupils to *imagine* what they can see through it. Waller (1978) describes a clock face with movable hands for teaching time expressions. This also benefits from having the circular clock face defined by a cardboard surround.

There is a limit to the pedagogical effect of sheet silhouettes, however. I did once go so far as to make a silhouette of the British Isles, with opaque sea and transparent land, so that other details could be added to it. This is both reusable and effective, and I do not begrudge the few hours it took to make. But people do tend to gasp and ask how it was made, instead of concentrating on the information it is supposed to present. So one can go too far.

It is often a good idea to stick a sheet of acetate to the upper side of these sheet silhouettes to give a smooth working surface for the movement of other elements in a display. For instance, you can make an effective *window*, as in Figure 62. Pictures of items of new vocabulary (e.g. animals) can be passed across it at varying speeds and heights, while you ask, *What's this?* or *What was that?* or *What's next, do you think?* Without acetate on top of the sheet silhouette it would be difficult to move the animals smoothly, unless you put them on the acetate roll, in which case you could not vary the order of presentation. With an acetate sheet, there is the additional advantage that one can make the window bars of opaque tape and stick them straight on to the acetate sheet, instead of having to cut each separate window pane out of cardboard.

In short, silhouettes are extremely effective on the overhead projector. Their only disadvantage is that, being opaque, you cannot superimpose one upon another unless you want to turn the display into a *guessing game* which of course you may.

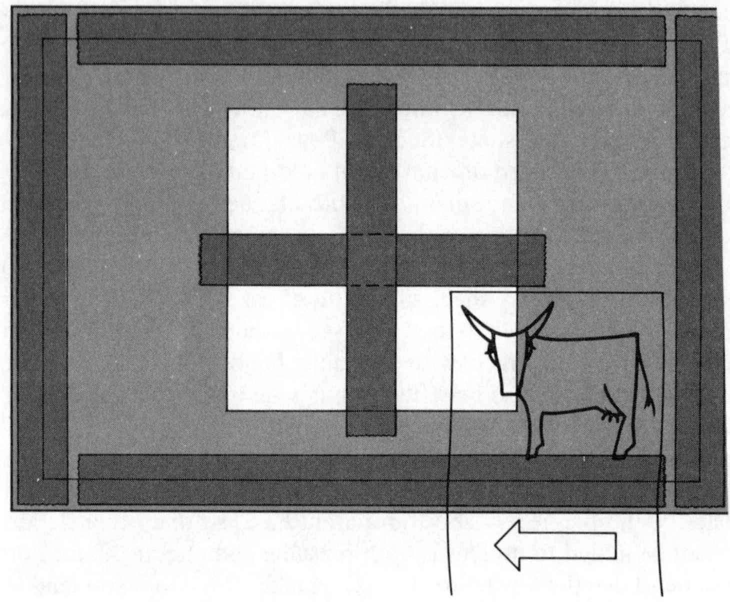

Figure 62 Silhouette window
Cut square hole in mask. Divide 'window' with opaque tape. Tape acetate sheet over whole mask. Slide acetate strips past window at different speeds and heights, asking, 'What's this?' *etc. (From an idea by students at Elverum Teacher Training College, Norway.)*

10 *Slide Mounts*

We have seen that small images can be moved around on the surface of a bigger transparency. The small images need not be silhouettes; they can also be transparencies. But very small transparencies need some extra protection if they are not to get damaged or lost.

A convenient answer is to mount a small transparency in a photographic slide holder. These holders come in a number of standard sizes. Apertures of 24 × 36 mm (as in Figure 63), or bigger, are suitable for use with the overhead projector. But 18 × 24 mm or 'half frame' slide holders are too small to be useful.

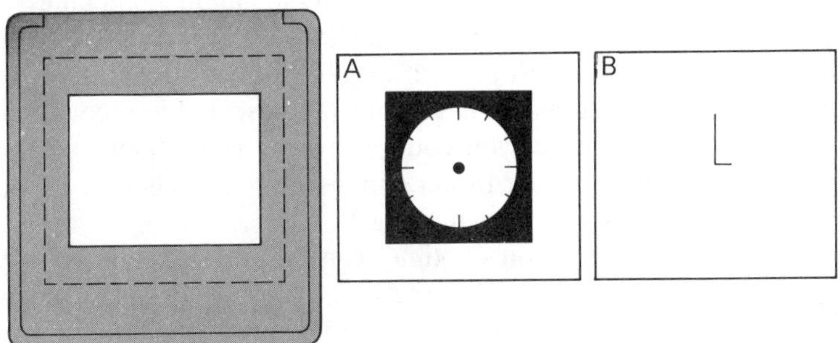

Figure 63 Clock in slide holder
Mount 'A' first. 'B' protects 'A' and clock hands can be redrawn in water-based ink.

The mounts are made of cardboard or plastic. Self-adhesive cardboard mounts are cheaper, and they are quite strong enough for normal purposes. Plastic mounts sometimes have the advantage that you can prise them open and reuse them with other transparencies: this depends on the design.

Slide holders can be stored in the various files and boxes designed for storing photographic transparencies. There are ring binders with translucent pages, each of which holds twenty slides. These are convenient because you can scan a page and select the slide you want without handling the others.

The obvious disadvantage of slide holders is that the mount itself is projected in silhouette. Glass 35 mm plates or microscope slides are sometimes used instead, but the introduction of glass means extra problems of storage, scratching and breakage. I use plastic mounts for abstract symbols which are small, and which do not need to be an integral part of the larger picture. The frame is not a nuisance in these cases.

The clock in Figure 63 is a good example. This is not for learning to tell the time – it is too small for that – but it is for giving an abstract *indication* of time. You cut two small rectangles of acetate to fit the mount. One is drawn in a permanent ink, and shows the clock face, and a spot in the centre. The other goes into the mount on top of the clock face, and protects it from damage. Any time you want to use the clock, simply draw in the hands with a water-based pen, centred on the permanent spot. The hands are easily erasable. There is no need to open the mount again unless a curious colleague has asked to see the 'innards'. (Note: some slide holders are supplied with glass inserts to protect the two sides of the photographic transparency. One of these holders could be used for the clock face: you could draw the clock hands on the glass instead. But they are rather expensive, so it is cheaper to use an acetate insert of your own making.)

This abstract indication of 'time' can be put into any picture. Weather can be indicated in the same way. Slides of a snow crystal, the sun, an umbrella, etc., can be moved round on a map of Europe, for instance, to practise those odd beginners' sentences:

It's fine in Moscow, but it's raining in London, etc.

The ice-cream symbol in Figure 37 would be one of a series of shops to be used in conjunction with maps on sheet transparencies.

The mounts in Figure 64 show various occupations. They can be used above the heads of all-purpose figures to provide rapid practice:

He's a teacher.
She's a doctor.
They're footballers.
He's going to be a baker, etc.

The symbols do not have to be definitively clear. Even if you have to explain them once, or the class has to guess (good practice for them, although perhaps uncomplimentary to your draughtsmanship), they are reusable, and recognizable, thereafter. These convenient abstractions are put into context in the following chapter.

Figure 64 Slide mounts of 'professions'

11 *Acetate Strips*

Hitherto the examples of transparencies have been largely *static*, albeit with elements added and concealed, and with the possibility of movement in silhouettes and slide mounts on the surface of the transparency. Yet it has also been stated that the overhead projector shares with the various 'pictureboards' the advantage that elements can not only be added and subtracted; they can be *moved* in relation to each other. To exploit this advantage, the picture we are projecting must be 'cut up' into its constituent parts. And as the example from *Britain Today* showed (see Figure 23), if this is done with imagination, we can *release* the elements from their relation to each other, and make each element reusable in a wider range of situations.

Suppose, for example, that you wished to present the situation in Figure 65 on the overhead projector, in order to involve the class more closely than is possible when they are being spoon-fed from the textbook. One has first to reduce the pictures to those elements which are essential to the story, as follows. Two *places* must be identified: station and bar. Two *male figures* are needed. You could either trace 'Ken' and 'George' from the textbook itself (you might already have them on acetate if they had appeared earlier in the course), or you could use any two other male figures in your files. An *official* is also needed: it is not necessary to make a distinction between the Attendant and the Porter. So one figure in a uniform is necessary. The only other *essential* element is the clock, which we constructed in the last chapter.

This gives us the six elements in Figure 66, all of which are obviously reusable elsewhere. We can now introduce the story bit by bit, at the class's own speed. We can either work straight towards the textbook passage, or we can ask the class to invent

1

GEORGE: Twó retúrn tíckets to Lóndon pléase.
Whát tíme will the néxt tráin léave?
ATTENDANT: At níneteen mínutes pást éight.

2

GEORGE: Whích plátform?
ATTENDANT: Plátform Twó.
Óver the brídge.

3

KEN: Whát tíme will the néxt tráin léave?
GEORGE: At éight ninetéen.
KEN: Wé've got plénty of tíme.

4

George: It's ónly thrée mínutes to eight.
KEN: Let's gó and háve a drínk.
Thére's a bár
néxt dóor to the státion.

5

GEORGE: Wé had bétter
gó báck to the státion now, Kén.

6

PORTER: Tíckets pléase.
GEORGE: We wánt to cátch
the éight ninetéen to Lóndon.
PORTER: You've júst missed it!

7

GEORGE: Whát!
It's ónly éight fiftéen.
PORTER: I'm sórry, sír.
Thát clóck's tén mínutes slów.
GEORGE: Whén's the néxt tráin?
PORTER: In fíve hóurs' tíme!

Figure 65 Example of illustrated dialogue
(From L. G. Alexander First Things First *(Longman, 1967) Lesson 95.)*

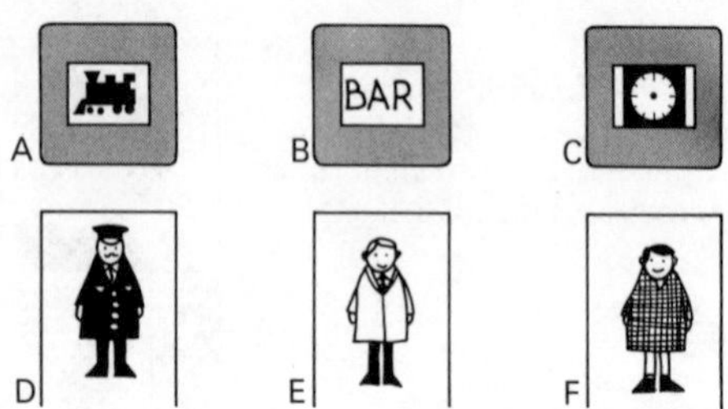

Figure 66 Elements of the story in Figure 65

their own tale from the 'cast' of these six elements (rather as Norman Davies suggests in 'Tell a Story', where groups are given six *phrases* in different orders, and required to weave a story round them: Davies, 1980).

For example, project Slide A (or the symbol of your local transport system). Ask, *Where is this?* (*At a station/Something to do with railways*/etc.) Add Strip D. *Who's this then, do you think?* (*The station-master*. Fine: we are not going to quibble about his status, because it is more important that each student contribution is *respected*.) And so on.

Ken and George can be moved across the screen to the bar (or coffee bar if you prefer: the choice is now in your hands):

Where are they going to now?
Why? What have they decided?

(To show they are *inside* the bar, simply *reverse* the bar sign!)

Having invented a story with class help, you can 'perform' the textbook version while listening to a tape of the textbook dialogue. If this is your aim, the cast and vocabulary will now be familiar. Or you can compare the textbook version with the version the class invented, and ask the students to point out the differences. Or groups of pupils themselves can study the textbook dialogue and devise an overhead projector 'performance' to go with it.

Whatever your aim, you can go at your own speed. You can reorganize or flashback at any stage. You can watch the class's faces and gauge their interest and comprehension. They will be even more involved if they make the figures themselves. They only need advice on keeping the figures clear and simple.

The figures can be used in 'puppet shows' such as the one described above, either from the textbook or devised by the pupils themselves. Or an interesting variant is to ask groups to create television or cinema commercials. Dialogue, music and 'noises off' go on a cassette tape: the visual side is illustrated on the overhead projector with transparencies made by the pupils themselves. This is a stimulating alternative to role play, and can result in some very professional presentations. The main thing is to explain the task clearly, and to give sufficient preparation time.

11.1 DESIGN AND STORAGE

The figures are easy to make. Standard acetate sheets are cut into parallel strips. In the account which follows, A4 sheets are cut into six equal strips, each 21 cm long and about 5 cm wide. These dimensions are convenient because the strips can be used horizontally for writing, and vertically for individual figures.

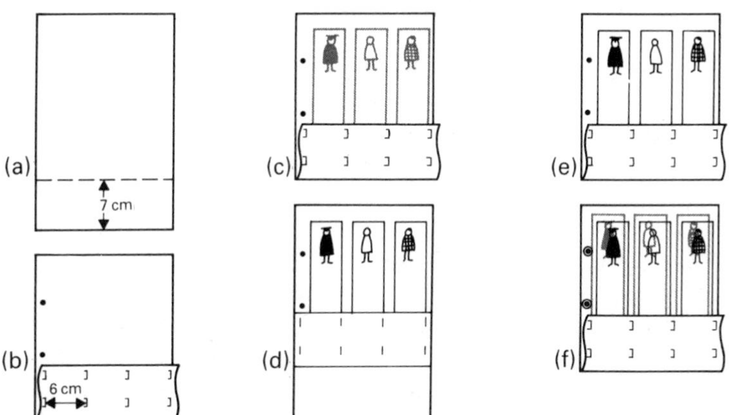

Figure 67 Filing acetate strips
(a) *Fold an ordinary sheet of A4 paper.*
(b) *Punch and staple.*
(c) *Photocopy folder complete with three acetate strips.*
(d) *Photocopy looks like this.*
(e) *Make a new folder from photocopy.*
(f) *File strips and reinforce punch holes.*

Storage is not a problem if the strips are cut to a standard size. File the strips as follows. First take a plain sheet of ordinary A4 paper (or whatever size suits your acetate strips). Make a fold 7 cm from the bottom and staple as in Figure 67. This sheet holds three 5 × 21 cm strips. Punch holes and use gummed reinforcements for filing in an ordinary ring binder.

Now comes the clever part. When you have collected three acetate strips in your new folder, *photocopy* them, *in the folder.* Make a new folder from the photocopy. This is very easy, because the holes and staples are now marked for you. Transfer the three strips to their new folder. Keep the blank holder for new strips. Any extra information, e.g. the name and source of a textbook figure, can be written on the folder.

This is a pretty foolproof way of filing the strips. It is quicker to make than to describe. You can build up a reference library of strips designed by you and your pupils.

11.2 INDIVIDUAL FIGURES

In Chapter 4, I said that the figures should be about 6 cm high. They should occupy the top third of the acetate strip. The rest should be left blank, so that you can manipulate figures at the centre of the glass screen on the overhead projector without the silhouette of your hand appearing distractingly. Bigger elements on the same scale, like the car in Figure 68, may need wider strips. They can be stored in the same kind of folder: just leave out one set of staples.

Trace or enlarge suitable figures from your textbook. (Advice on enlarging is given in Chapter 4: see Figures 24 and 25.) The most suitable figures are standing, looking to right or left (it does not matter which, because they are reversible). It helps if they are wearing 'neutral' clothes which are not exclusive to a particular place or season, to indoors or outdoors.

If you use coloured backdrops (see Chapter 5), draw your figures in a black or dark blue line without filling (i.e. without solid blocks of colour). Then they will show up clearly on coloured backgrounds.

Once traced or created, the characters can be shown in any

situation. With a bit of imagination, even a standing figure can be shown in bed (see Figure 69).

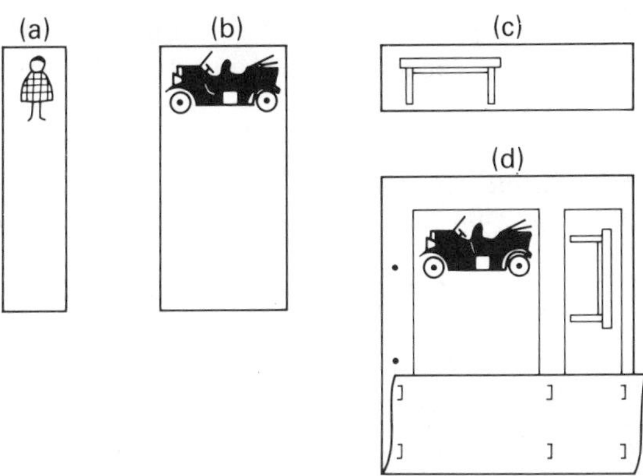

Figure 68 Larger pictures to standard scale
(a) *Standard size strip, 21 cm × 5 cm.*
(b) *Double-width strip, 21 cm × 10 cm.*
(c) *Standard strip: picture drawn sideways.*
(d) *Filing a double-width strip.*

Figure 69 Superimposing transparencies
Note that head of bed is left clear, while remainder is heavily shaded to conceal body.

Many activities normally associated with *flashcards* are conveniently presented with acetate strips. For example, vocabulary can be practised with the 'Going Away' game (Lee, 1979). Display six to eight new items next to a suitcase, as in Figure 70. Slide each one into the case as each pupil adds to the ever-lengthening sentence:

I'm going to (London) and I'll take a suitcase, a toothbrush, a pair of socks and some soap with me.

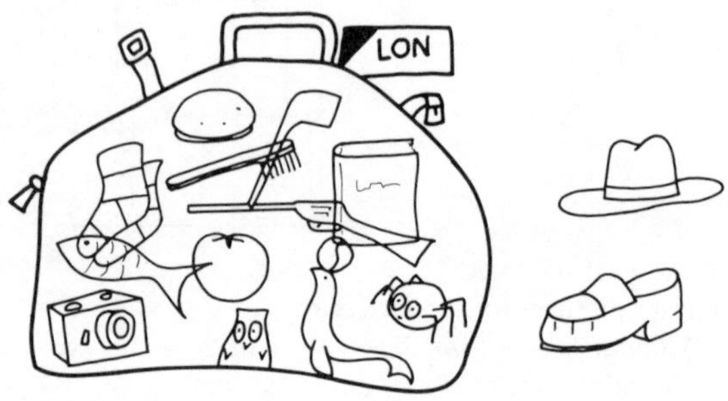

Figure 70 'Going Away' game
(From W. R. Lee, Language Teaching Games and Contests *(OUP, 1979).)*

Alternatively, make the suitcase an opaque silhouette and hide the new items in there, asking students to guess 'what's in the bag'. Even with a transparent suitcase, six pictures (or even more especially, words) *superimposed* will make this quite enough of a guessing game.

Another possibility is to practise *minimal pairs*. Use a background transparency with colour circles, or two maps, for example. On this, place acetate strips of *familiar* objects with similar names (like *ship* and *sheep*). The class instruct a student at the projector:

Put the ship in the green circle.
Send the sheep to England.

or whatever is relevant to the picture.

11.3 WRITING

Words or phrases can also be put on strips. For the latter, turn the strip sideways. You can write on the whole strip, because you are not going to need to be a puppeteer, as with the individual figures.

For example, scatter five words on separate strips on the projector top. Project them briefly: e.g. *ready, your, is, nearly, dinner.* Ask the class to put them into a sentence. The first individual or team to answer can demonstrate the sentence on the projector:

your dinner is nearly ready

In the same way, Kim's Word Game (Lee, 1979) is conveniently played on the overhead projector. The words are projected and students then write down, or put into sentences, as many as they can remember and spell. They should, of course, be familiar words.

Sentences or lines of poetry can be ordered in the same way, again with a time limit on the projection and/or the solution time. If you think you might forget the correct order of the lines or sentences yourself, stick an opaque circle on each acetate strip, and note the order there (see Figure 71, with lines from *Under Milk Wood*).

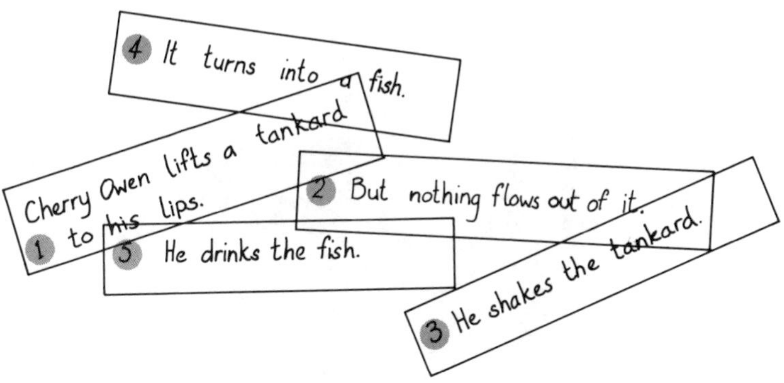

Figure 71 Sentences on acetate strips

Another possibility is to get half the class to make word strips beginning with *If I had* . . . and the other half with *I would have* . . . Call pairs out at random to combine their phrases on the projector, and see if the combinations make any sense (see Figure 72).

'Consequences' (e.g. Lee, 1979) can be played in the same way.

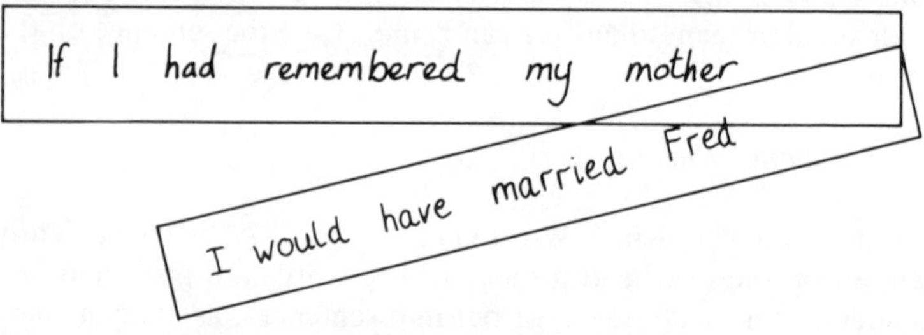

Figure 72 Combining strips written by pupils

Figure 73 Commutation frame
'He hates bread'.

11.4 SUBSTITUTION TABLES

Prepare three or four acetate strips, and on each strip draw three alternative pictures as in Figure 73. Place these on a 'commutation frame' (Jones, 1978). This is a mounted acetate sheet covered with translucent colour film apart from a slot, 7 cm high, right across the centre of the frame. This is left blank.

In Figure 73, you will see that one of a number of possible sentences is illustrated in the centre slot. The class can see the other possibilities on each strip, through the colour film. They can therefore decide which sentence they want next. If you would prefer each sentence to be a surprise, simply use an opaque frame.

The individual strips are reusable in other combinations. They provide rapid practice in substitutions. The three strips in Figure 73 provide illustration for twenty-seven sentences. An extra three-picture strip would raise the possibilities to 3^4, or eighty-one sentences.

In some constructions, though not the one illustrated, there is the further possibility of changing the *order* of the strips to symbolize a transformational relationship. *(He's) giving (her) the (bread)* becomes *(He's) giving the (bread) to (her)*, for instance.

11.5 SUMMARY

Once the storage problem has been solved through standardization, acetate strips provide a very flexible system for exploiting the overhead projector in as many ways as you can think of.

12 *Combinations*

This chapter is an assortment of the following sorts of combination:

(a) Two conventions within a single image, particularly combinations of words and pictures.
(b) Two or more techniques in one image: a summary.
(c) The overhead projector and other aids.

12.1 COMBINING CONVENTIONS

It will be clear that there is no objection to mixing words and pictures on the overhead projector. Sentences can be illustrated very nicely with pictures for the more concrete items and words for the more abstract items, just as in Figure 73. Depending on the kind of class you teach, you might like to think about other aspects of the combination of words and pictures. Words, letters and numbers can be made more 'picture-like' for younger children (rather in the manner of 'Sesame Street', the American educational programme). The results can be attractive and memorable (see Figure 74).

Figure 74 'Picture-like' symbols
'How many apples are there?'

Conversely, pictures can be made more 'word-like'. Allen and Valette (1972), for instance, suggest blackboard *ideograms* (see Figure 75). These can be elaborated for the overhead projector (as in Figure 76), because they can be drawn in advance and reused later.

Figure 75 Blackboard ideograms
'He's going to the baker's.' (After Allen and Valette, 1972.)

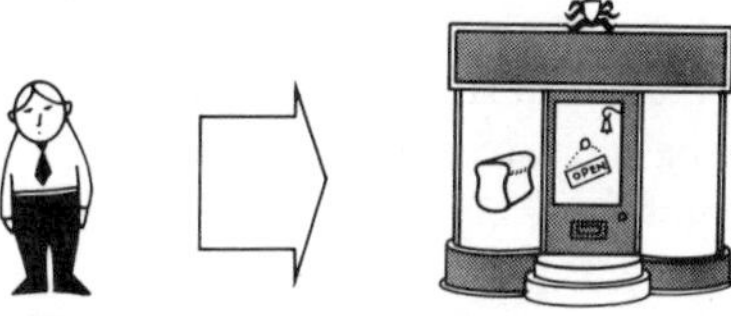

Figure 76 Acetate strips used as ideograms
The shopfront is reusable. The bread sign is superimposed on it.

Figure 77 Time lines combined with illustrations

Other symbols can be brought into play. There are conventions such as the 'time lines' which many teachers use, interestingly developed by Doug Case (1978). If a time line, symbolising a particular tense in English, is drawn on a sheet transparency, space can be left for illustration of the structure by figures on acetate strips, as in Figure 77:

Tense: present perfect continuous.
Examples: *I've been asking her to marry me for twenty years.*
I've been feeding Pussy for twenty years.

Other combinations will occur as long as you follow the basic principle of making each element *reusable.*

12.2 COMBINING TECHNIQUES

It will also be clear that to get the most out of an overhead projector it is necessary to combine all the techniques at one's disposal as imaginatively as you can. Masks, silhouettes, sheet transparencies and acetate strips can all be thrown in together.

Just to make these combinations explicit, here is an example to summarize the possibilities. The starting point is a presentation of the contrast between the functions of the simple and continuous past tenses in sentences like:

What was the old lady doing when the rain came?
What did the old lady do when the rain came?

(See *Kernel Lessons Intermediate*, page 94, for the origins of this presentation.)

The picture might be built up as follows.

(a) Background. A park. Either a sheet transparency, drawn or photocopied, or a more abstract indication, such as a green backdrop, plus a tree, seat, flowers, perhaps an ice-cream shop, etc. The latter can be on acetate strips or drawn *in situ*.
(b) Characters. Introduce figures on acetate strips, asking the class:
What's he/she doing?
(He's walking towards the seat.)
(She's looking at the flowers.)

(c) When the park is fully populated, introduce an *overlay* of heavy rain, and immediately turn off the projector. Ask:
What was the old lady doing when the rain came?
And later:
What do you think the old lady did when the rain came?
(*Ran under a tree/hid in the ice-cream shop*/etc.)

(d) Get groups to construct complete narratives describing this situation. Then they demonstrate their narratives with overhead projector accompaniments.

Two other details. After turning off the projector at (c), put the overlay of rain *under* the backdrop of the park. The projected image will look exactly the same when you turn it back on again, but you will be able to move about the acetate strips in accordance with the pupils' answers to your questions. Secondly, *Kernel Lessons Intermediate* uses other 'natural disasters' to dramatize this kind of sentence. For example, a King Kong figure appears at a banquet. This is very appealing for a younger class, of course. King Kong can easily be represented by a large *silhouette*, such as an Indonesian shadow puppet, or some home-made monster.

There are other examples of combinations of this kind throughout this book. Once you have built up some kind of software armoury, if that is the right phrase, the possibilities are immense.

12.3 COMBINING THE OVERHEAD PROJECTOR WITH OTHER AIDS

Ways in which the overhead projector can be used to focus attention on aspects of a *textbook* passage or *handout* have already been mentioned:

(a) The passage can be photocopied on to a transparency.
(b) Comprehension questions or key words can be presented on the overhead projector and revealed one by one with a mask.
(c) A passage can be dramatized on the overhead projector, through the use of small figures on acetate strips.

The same methods can be used with a passage on *tape*. If the passage has a lot of different speakers, put a character on the overhead projector to represent each speaker, and simply wiggle that character whenever he speaks. This can be a great help to understanding the tape. The overhead projector performance can be repeated later in the lesson, without the tape, as a guide to pupils retelling the story.

With the *blackboard*, pictures on the overhead projector combine very well with words on the board, as long as it is possible for the class to see both at the same time.

Lighter surfaces can be used as overhead projection screens in the following ways.

If the overhead projector is projected on to the surface of a *whiteboard* (or a sheet of white paper attached to blackboard or wall), additions can be made on the board as well as the projector. For example, you could draw the time line in Figure 77 on the whiteboard, as part of your presentation of the associated tense. You could switch on the overhead projector in the later practice phase, projecting your acetate strips on to the whiteboard, above the time line.

If the overhead projector shines on to a white *magnetboard,* you could give your magnetboard characters the range of projected backgrounds that the overhead projector provides.

If you project on to a *wallchart* or *map,* you can make additions on the projector without dirtying the chart. For instance, you could people a map of Britain with overhead projector characters, or you could draw attention to certain areas of a wallchart with colour circles on the projector.

The summit of this kind of combination would be the opportunity to project *slides*, which would provide the realism and full colour that the overhead projector cannot offer, and then to be able to use the full range of overhead projector techniques to exploit the slide picture. There is one very expensive overhead projector (the ITM Diascribe 800D), which has a slide projector in the base, but I have not been able to lay my hands on one to see how well one can combine the two techniques.

A number of manufacturers offer slide *attachments* for overhead projectors. This usually means that the slide attachment uses the same light source, or the same projection lenses, as the overhead projector, but one cannot project transparencies and slides at the same time. The attachments I have seen have not been very impressive projectors of slides, either.

To return to some more basic aids: the overhead projector is often an effective *replacement* for various kinds of wall-hung material. For instance, there are those large composite primary school murals where each pupil has made an animal, and they are all stuck together on to a huge green jungle. The overhead projector offers a stage for composite pictures which can be adjusted, or even animated. Each element is drawn by a different pupil on a piece of acetate. If you teach in one of those nomadic schools where no class is ever in the same room for two lessons running, there is the advantage that you can pack up the whole picture at the end of the lesson, and keep it safe for the next meeting.

Games like darts and 'Tail on the Donkey' can be dramatically and *safely* transferred to the overhead projector. Make sheet transparencies of a dartboard or a donkey, and throw lumps of plasticine at them from great distances. Or, for more *language* practice, blindfold the players and have them *place* (not throw) the darts or donkey tail, with loud and conflicting instructions from the rest of the class.

In summary, it is very easy to do without an overhead projector, of course. But if you have one in your classroom, there are endless ways in which techniques you associate with other aids can fruitfully be converted to include the projector.

13 *Specialist Transparencies and Movement*

The point of the book so far has been that overhead projector visuals are worth making if they can be used and reused in a wide range of situations. In other words, they should be simple and general. In turning now to visuals which are neither simple nor general, I propose merely the following:

(a) To outline the wealth of commercially available transparencies for specialist use.
(b) To describe some techniques for the projection of movement which might interest the ESP teacher. I cannot myself think of any 'straight EFL uses for these techniques, but the reader can judge for himself.

13.1 SPECIALIST TRANSPARENCIES

The Leybold-Heraeus catalogue describes experiments designed for the overhead projector in bewildering variety. Not only is movement created by electric motors, strobes, and old-fashioned turning of handles, but there is even an air blower which sets up an area of negligible friction within a frame on the projection stage. There is a pair of magnetic coils that completely enclose the sides of the projector, for experiments with iron filings (which project very nicely, incidentally). Leybold–Heraeus also have a system of mirrors whereby 450 different vertical test-tube experiments can be projected from an ordinary horizontal stage. (The alternative system is to buy a projector where the whole projection stage can be rotated to the vertical for the projection of test-tube experiments.) There are colour-mixing demonstrations that would require a far more finely tuned projector than anything we need in the language classroom. In short, the overhead projector is seen as the light source for an astonishing array of demonstration experiments, designed to be seen by everyone in the room.

It is interesting to look through the catalogues just to see the display techniques that are used. Many of the commercially produced models consist of clear plexiglass bases, for instance, on which coloured translucent parts slide, or rotate on studs (see Figure 78). These models have to be machined in thick plastic, almost as carefully as the real thing. An alternative is to *use* the real thing if it is flat, like the gearing in Figure 78. Companies like ESA produce a range of *transparent pinboards* (see Figure 79), which could be used as reusable bases for such working models. The projecting pins would serve as axles for (opaque silhouetted) gears from Meccano, or similar construction sets.

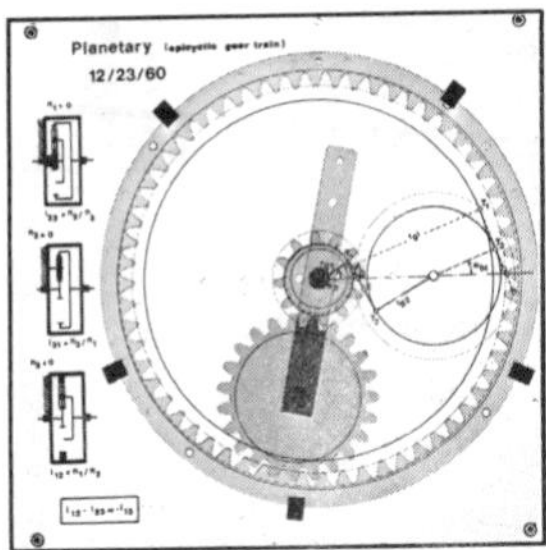

Figure 78 Planetary gear (Leybold-Heraeus)

Figure 79 Translucent pinboards (ESA)

Talking of the 'real thing', it is worth mentioning that the whole range of protractors, set squares and curves used in *technical drawing* project very nicely, as long as the calibrations are clear.

A number of interesting visual effects can be produced in a *water tray*, i.e. a transparent dish, preferably the same size as the projection stage, containing water. Even clear water casts a shadow which can be used in showing wave effects. The British Council film *The Overhead Projector* illustrates the use of a perspex 'ripple tank' with lint baffles around the edges to damp the wave action (see Figure 80).

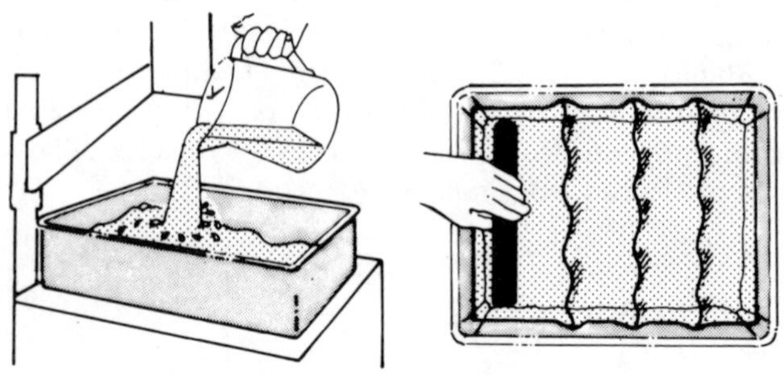

Figure 80 Ripple tank to illustrate wave action
(From British Council film, The Overhead Projector. *Diagram from Wilkinson, 1979, p. 30.)*

Apart from the catalogues, there are a number of specialist texts on overhead projection. (Full references are given in the reference section.)

Chemistry: Alyea, 1963; and Hartung, 1953.

Medicine: McRae, 1971a; and McRae, 1975. I have already cited the latter because it contains a lot of good general points, especially on selecting a projector.

Maths: Krulik and Kaufman, 1966. This is another good general introduction to overhead projection techniques.

Geography: Best, 1968. This is very wordy, but good on the technology of the overhead projector.

Other school subjects: Schultz, 1965. Many good ideas, but you have to read through every subject section to find them.

13.2 MOVEMENT THROUGH POLARIZATION

An impression of *flow* can be created with a *polarizing spinner* (see Figure 81), attached to the lens assembly. The same effect is provided by an *animation roll* (such as Opasym), fitted in place of the normal acetate roll. With either system, self-adhesive *movement patterns* must be attached to the areas of the transparency where the impression of flow is required. Manual and motorized versions of both systems are available. The main function is to give an impression of movement through a system. The bloodstream, hydraulic brakes and radiation are topics that come to mind.

If you would rather make your own polarizing spinner, McRae (1972) tells you how.

Figure 81 Polarising spinner

13.3 MOVEMENT THROUGH ARTICULATION

The construction of *working models* for the overhead projector is a study in itself. Powell (1964) and McRae (1971b) provide useful introductions. McRae (1968) also describes the construction of a model of the musco-skeletal system, using rubber bands for muscles. The principles of construction are applicable to other models. *The Overhead Projector*, the British Council instructional film (which is very good), features a model steam-engine built along similar lines. The flexible bits are rubber bands, and the inflexible bits are silhouetted (see Figure 82).

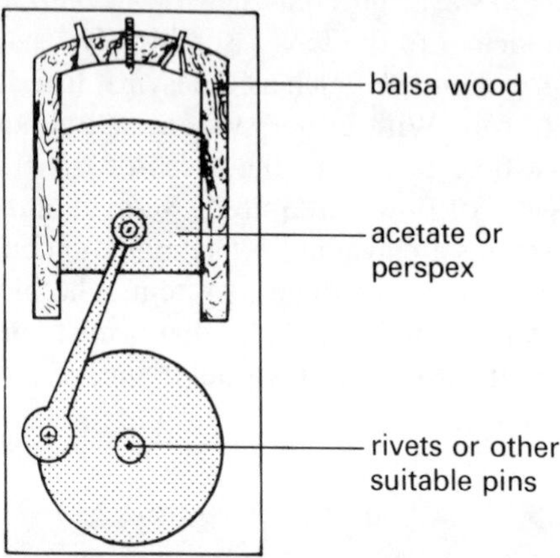

Figure 82 Model steam engine
(Diagram from Wilkinson, 1979, p. 30.)

The advantage of opaque parts in home-made models is that the joins (of rubber bands and cardboard) are concealed, and the various fulcrums are invisible, so everything looks neater.

The possibilities are intriguing of course, and rewarding, but unfortunately they lie outside the purview of this book. The more elaborate the model, the more limited its use. On the other hand, the place for this kind of model in courses of many kinds is clear. As McRae (1975) points out, if technical transparencies of various kinds are used consistently to illustrate a course, a student who misses a lesson can later go to the projector file and take out the work he has missed. He can then study it on his own, without needing the projector itself.

Appendix: Where to Obtain Equipment

TRAINING FILMS

The Overhead Projector (British Council), 16 mm colour, 25 minutes (English and Arabic versions available).
Suppliers:
(Sales or hire)
Guild Sound and Vision Ltd
Woodston House
Oundle Road
Peterborough PE2 9PZ
Telephone: 0733 63122

(Sales only)
Printing and Publishing Department
The British Council
65 Davies Street
London W1Y 2AA
Telephone: 01 499 8011

(Or contact your local British Council office.)

Over to You (Arbor Films/Educational Foundation for Visual Aids), 16 mm colour, 26 minutes (also on video cassette).

Suppliers:
National Audio-Visual Aids Library
Paxton Place
Gipsy Road
London SE27 9SR
Telephone: 01 670 4247

MATERIALS MENTIONED IN THIS BOOK

(UK suppliers unless otherwise mentioned)

Bell & Howell Audio-Visual Ltd
Alperton House
Bridgewater Road
Wembley
Middlesex HA0 1EG
machines, materials, Cellobinder storage system

Elite Optics Ltd
Gnome Corner
354 Caerphilly Road
Cardiff CF4 4XJ
machines, materials

ESA Creative Learning Ltd
Pinnacles
PO Box 22
Harlow
Essex CM19 5AY
transparent pinboards

International Tutor Machines Ltd
15 Holder Road
Aldershot
Hants GU12 4RH
projectors, copiers, materials

Letraset (UK) Ltd
St George's House
195–203 Waterloo Road
London SE1 8XJ
materials, especially lettering

Leybold-Heraeus GmbH & Co
Scientific and Technical Education Division
Postfach 51 07 60
D-5000 Köln 51
West Germany
machines, trolleys, scientific materials

3M (UK) Ltd
63 Croydon Road
London SE20 7TS
projectors, copiers, materials

Ofrex Ltd
Ofrex House
Stephen Street
London W1A 1EA
projectors, copiers, materials

Pennant Audio-Visual Systems
Lansdown Place Lane
Cheltenham
Glos. GL50 2LA
polarising systems, scientific materials

Rexel Ltd
Gatehouse Road
Aylesbury
Bucks. HP19 3DT
copiers, mounts, materials

Smith, G. H. & Partners Ltd (Sales)
Berechurch Road
Colchester
Essex
Pelikan pens

Staedtler (UK) Ltd
Pontyclun
Mid-Glamorgan CF7 8YJ
materials

Swan-Stabilo Ltd
71 Parkway
Camden Town
London NW1 7QJ
materials

Technamation Ltd
101 Bell Street
Reigate
Surrey
polarising systems, materials

Transaid
Francis Gregory & Son Ltd
Spur Road
Feltham
Middlesex TW14 0SX
polarising systems, materials

Transart Visual Products
East Chadley Lane
Godmanchester
Cambs. PE18 8AU
Diazo materials, Opasym animators, Flipatran storage system, other materials

Information on machines and materials, including a full list of suppliers of overhead projector material for other subjects, is available from:
National Committee for Audio-Visual Aids in Education
Paxton Place
Gipsy Road
London SE27 9SR

References

Allen, E. D., and Valette, R. M., *Modern Language Classroom Techniques* (Harcourt Brace Jovanovich, 1972), p. 164.

Alyea, H. N., *'Tops': Tested Overhead Projection Series* (Journal of Chemical Education, 1963).

Bell & Howell, *How to Use Your Overhead Projector* (Bell & Howell, 1968).

Best, T. D., *Geography via the Overhead Projector* (National Council for Geographic Education, Illinois State University, 1968).

Brims, J., 'Using the overhead projector', in Holden (1978), pp. 58-63. See Holden.

Broughton, G., *Success with English,* Coursebook 2 (Penguin, 1969), p. 96.

Burkart, E. I., 'The check procedure in a technical English training course', *English Teaching Forum,* vol. 18, no. 2 (1980), pp. 29–32.

Case, D., 'Time lines – 2', in Moorwood (1978), pp. 22-3. See Moorwood.

Davies, N. F., 'Oral fluency training and small groups', *English Teaching Forum,* vol. 18, no. 3 (1980), pp. 36–9.

EFL Gazette, 'A devil's dictionary of EFL', *EFL Gazette* (June, 1980).

Elgar, R., and Rees, A., 'West Winghythe – a versatile visual', in Holden (1978), pp. 33-7. See Holden.

English Teaching Forum, 'Crossing the bridge', *English Teaching Forum,* vol. 18, no. 7 (1980), p. 48. (The solution to the problem on page 62 is that Alfonso is a juggler: while he is crossing the bridge, there is always one pineapple in the air.)

Harrison, K. M., 'Enlarging small pictures', in Moorwood (1978), pp. 75–6. See Moorwood.

Hartung, E. J., *The Screen Projection of Chemical Experiments* (Melbourne University Press, 1953).

Holden, S. (ed.), *Visual Aids for Classroom Interaction* (Modern English Publications, 1978).

Jones, J. R. H., 'Getting the most out of an overhead projector', *English Language Teaching Journal,* vol. 32, no. 3 (1978), pp. 194–201.

Kerr, J. Y. K., 'Silhouette images and the overhead projector', part 1, *Modern English Teacher,* vol. 6, no. 3 (1978a), pp. 15–16.

Kerr, J. Y. K., 'Silhouette images and the overhead projector', part 2, *Modern English Teacher,* vol. 6, no. 4 (1978b), pp. 16–18.

Kodak, *Preparing Transparencies for the Overhead Projector* (available from: Kodak Ltd, 190, High Holborn, London WC1V 7AE).

Krulik, S., and Kaufman, I., *How to Use the Overhead Projector in Mathematics Education* (National Council of Teachers of Mathematics, Inc., 1966).

Langer, Z., 'The overhead projector: some new suggestions', *English Teaching Guidance,* no. 23 (1972), pp. 18–22.

Lee, W. R., *Language Teaching Games and Contests,* 2nd ed., (OUP, 1979).

Leggat, R., *Lights Please!* (National Committee for Audio-Visual Aids in Education, 1972).

McBride, O., *The Overhead Projector* (3M Educational Services Press, 1965).

McRae, R K., 'Working anatomical models for the overhead projector', *Medical and Biological Illustration,* vol. 18 no. 4 (1968), pp. 249–52.

McRae, R. K., *How to Use the Overhead Projector* (Medical Recording Service Foundation, 1971a). This booklet, and the tape and slides which it accompanies, are available from MRSF at Kitts Croft, Writtle, Chelmsford, Essex, England (catalogue no. 71/56).

McRae, R. K., *Working Models for the Overhead Projector* (Medical Recording Service Foundation 1971b). Available with tape and slides from the above address (catalogue no. 71/57).

McRae, R. K., 'A simple polarising spinner for the overhead projector', *Medical and Biological Illustration,* vol. 22, no. 3 (1972), pp. 191–3.

McRae, R. K., *The Overhead Projector* (Association for the Study of Medical Education, 1975).

Minnesota Mining and Manufacturing Company (3M), *Op Art* (1965). Later editions available from: 3M Co. Ltd, Marketing Dept, Business Communication Division, 3M House, Wigmore Street, London W1A 1ET.

Moorwood, H. (ed.), *Selections from Modern English Teacher* (Longman, 1978).

Moorwood, H., 'Picture problems', in Moorwood (1978), pp. 33—4. See above.

O'Neill, R., and Kingsbury, R., *Kernel Lessons Intermediate* (Longman, 1971), p. 94.

Powell, L. S., *A Guide to the Overhead Projector* (British Association for Commercial and Industrial Education, 1964).

Satchwell, R. H., *Overhead Projectors* (Audio-Visual Teaching Aids, 1972).

Schultz, M. J., *The Teacher and Overhead Projection* (Prentice-Hall, 1965).

Sivell, J., 'Self-correction of compositions: the three-pencil method', *English Teaching Forum,* vol. 18, no. 3 (1980), pp. 42–3.

Tecnifax, *Diazochrome Projectuals for Visual Communication* (Tecnifax Corp., 1963).

Waller, C., 'An illustrated guide to overhead projector software', in Holden (1978), pp. 64–8.

Wilkinson, J., *The Overhead Projector* (British Council, 1979).

Wright, A., 'Silhouetted images and the overhead projector', part 3, *Modern English Teacher,* vol, 6, no. 5 (1979a), pp. 15–16.

Wright, A., 'Silhouetted images and the overhead projector', part 4, *Modern English Teacher,* vol. 6, no. 6 (1979b), pp. 18–20.

Wright, A., Betteridge, B., and Buckby, M., *Games for Language Learning* (CUP, 1979).